THE MULTILATERAL DEVELOPMENT BANKS

VOLUME 3
THE CARIBBEAN DEVELOPMENT BANK

THE MULTILATERAL DEVELOPMENT BANKS

VOLUME 3
THE CARIBBEAN DEVELOPMENT BANK

CHANDRA HARDY

LYNNE RIENNER PUBLISHERS

THE NORTH-SOUTH INSTITUTE
L'INSTITUT NORD-SUD

Published in the United States of America in 1995 by
Lynne Rienner Publishers, Inc.
1800 30th Street, Boulder, Colorado 80301

and in the United Kingdom by
Lynne Rienner Publishers, Inc.
3 Henrietta Street, Covent Garden, London WC2E 8LU

Paperback edition published in Canada by
The North-South Institute
55 Murray Street
Ottawa, Ontario K1N 5M3 Canada

Library of Congress Cataloging-in-Publication Data
Multilateral development banks.
    p.   cm.
    Includes bibliographical references and index.
    Contents: — 3. The Caribbean Development Bank / by Chandra Hardy.
    ISBN 1-55587-469-X (alk. paper : v. 3)—
    ISBN 1-55587-495-9 (pbk. : alk. paper : v. 3)
    1. Development banks. 2. Caribbean Development Bank.
HG1975.M848 1995
332.2—dc20   94-45003
                                                                   CIP

Canadian Cataloguing in Publication Data
Main entry under title:
Multilateral development banks
    Includes bibliographical references.
    Contents: v. 3. The Caribbean Development Bank /
    by Chandra Hardy.
    ISBN 0-921942-80-X (v. 3)
    1. Development banks. I. North-South Institute
(Ottawa, Ont.)
HG1975.M85 1995   322.1'52   C95-900188-3

British Cataloguing in Publication Data
A Cataloguing in Publication record for this book
is available from the British Library.

CONTENTS

TABLES

FOREWORD

I am delighted to have been asked to contribute this foreword to Chandra Hardy's book on the Caribbean Development Bank (CDB) for three reasons: first, the timeliness and quality of the publication; second, the tremendous contribution the CDB has made and continues to make to the Caribbean in general and the OECS countries in particular; and third, my family's very close association with this most West Indian of institutions.

My first knowledge of the CDB was through my father, Noel Venner, who called me at the University of the West Indies in Mona, Jamaica, to inform me of yet another dislocation in the life of the Venner family in search of the holy grail of regional cooperation and unity. He had been engaged by the United Nations Development Programme to do the preliminary work for the establishment of this new institution. Our odyssey, which started in St. Vincent and had so far encompassed Grenada, St. Lucia, and Guyana, would continue to Barbados. Since I was studying economics and my father considered me a good listener, I was at the receiving end of unsolicited lectures on development banks in general and on what was going to be the greatest regional development bank in particular. I was made aware of the fact that the CDB was a triumph for the many regionalists who were undaunted by the demise of the West Indian Federation and were certain that the road to progress in the Caribbean lay in regional cooperation, even if not at the political level.

The CDB has lived up to its early billings and expectations. It has been fortunate to have had excellent leadership in its three presidents: first, Sir Arthur Lewis, Nobel laureate and repository of the hopes of the regional technocrats; second, William Demas, an ardent regionalist and intellectual protagonist for the special circumstances of small states; and currently, Sir Neville Nichols, whose long association with the institution and calm approach to its administration has brought it through the turmoil of recent years.

As a director of the CDB for many years, I have stressed the need for the institution to be mindful of its dual mandate: to maintain prudent banking policies and to be an initiator and catalyst for the development of its member states. This particular issue is not dead, as Chandra Hardy confirms, but one that my own institution has sought to define in a pragmatic way. We place strong emphasis on stability and prudent banking practices as a precursor for sustainable development, but we also see a strong role for institutions like the CDB to undertake focused research efforts in order to define a suitable development paradigm for its member states. This matter has engaged my attention since my first meeting with Sir Arthur Lewis, when, as a newly minted graduate of the University of the West Indies, I was presented to the great man by my father, who was then the Bank secretary. I remember Sir Arthur, with his head slightly inclined to one side, quizzing me on the development prospects of the OECS countries and explaining to me the role of the CDB in its regional context. It was one of the most stimulating conversations I have been privileged to have in my professional life.

Chandra Hardy has done an excellent job of chronicling the achievements of the CDB. Its contribution to the OECS countries is clearly demonstrated by the progress of these islands. The CDB is by far their largest provider of development finance, which is reflected in vital infrastructure and a constant replenishment of the project pipeline.

The Bank's involvement with first Guyana and then Grenada is important in signaling its commitment to the economic recovery of its member states and is a clear case of its role being beyond simply a bank. Its active participation in the Caribbean Group for Cooperation in Economic Development illustrates another vital role of the institution as an effective intermediary between the region on the one hand and multilateral institutions and the donor community on the other.

This publication appears at a critical period of West Indian economic history, as we are in transition from an era of protected markets and concessional aid flows to a more open and liberalized trading and financial environment and a drastic decline in aid to the region. We look to institutions like the CDB to play an active role in our transition. Chandra Hardy's book clearly outlines the situation of the region and the CDB and provides an excellent platform for the efforts that need to be made in the next phase of our development.

K. Dwight Venner
Governor, Eastern Caribbean Central Bank
St. Kitts-Nevis

PREFACE

In 1991 the North-South Institute launched its research project on the multilateral development banks ("the MDB Project"). The principal focus of the project was the group of regional development banks (comprising the African, Asian, and Inter-American Development Banks) plus the subregional Caribbean Development Bank. All these banks, created more or less in the image of the World Bank, had been around for two to three decades. Yet, in contrast to the World Bank, they had been subjected to little critical scrutiny.

The project was designed to provide a consistent framework within which each of the banks could be examined. Besides providing a brief history of the origins and evolution of its subject, each study reviews the experience of a selected group of borrowing countries, as well as the bank's performance as a lender and as a mobilizer of resources. In all of the studies, the operations and policies of the regional bank are compared with those of the World Bank; also addressed are relations between the two agencies and the division of labor between them. Finally, each study looks ahead at the challenges facing the banks in the future.

In a word, the studies seek to determine the *development effectiveness* of the regional banks by examining their impact on growth, poverty, the environment, and social indicators of development. It is hoped that the project will make an important contribution to ongoing discussions regarding the future of the multilateral system of development financing, now in its fiftieth year after the Bretton Woods Conference. In addition to this volume on the Caribbean Bank, the project will yield four other major publications—one each on the Inter-American, Asian, and African Banks, as well as a "synthesis" volume. There are also two studies on Canada's role in the MDBs, one on Sweden and the MDBs, and one on Jamaica's relations with the MDBs.

The project has been generously supported through grants

from the Canadian International Development Agency, the Inter-American Development Bank, the Asian Development Bank, the African Development Bank, the Ford Foundation, the Swedish Ministry for Foreign Affairs, the Caribbean Development Bank, the Norwegian Ministry of Foreign Affairs, and the Netherlands Ministry for Development Cooperation. The views contained in this volume and in others issuing from the project, however, are those of the authors alone and do not necessarily reflect the views of the project's sponsors, the funders of the multilateral development banks project, the North-South Institute, its supporters, or its board of directors.

Roy Culpeper
MDB Project Director
The North-South Institute

ACKNOWLEDGMENTS

This book is part of a larger study of the regional development banks undertaken by the North-South Institute. I would like to thank the North-South Institute and, in particular, Roy Culpeper, the director of the project, for inviting me to be a member of the team and for giving me wise counsel throughout.

I wish to acknowledge the extensive cooperation provided by the management and staff of the Caribbean Development Bank in carrying out this study. I am grateful for the encouragement and insights provided by Sir Neville Nichols, president of the CDB. Marius St. Rose, vice-president of operations, and Masie Plummer, vice-president of corporate services, were generous with their time for interviews. I cannot list all the staff who provided assistance, but I trust that they will recognize their contributions in the completed work. I do wish to mention and thank R. Mullins, N. Grainger, A. Eustace, D. Brunton, A. Maughn, J. Dellimore, W. Lawrence, K. Worrell, and Dorla Humes for the time spent discussing various aspects of the Bank's work. I also thank the staff of the library for their unfailing courtesy. I am especially indebted to Jasper Scotland, deputy director of policy and planning, who coordinated my work at the Bank, provided guidance at each stage, and gave detailed comments on an earlier draft.

I would like to thank Ione Marshall for her assistance in conducting research, compiling statistical information, and conducting interviews. The country studies draw on research provided by Sharon Singh for the OECS countries, Ione Marshall and Courtney Blackman for Barbados, and George Reid for Jamaica.

I have also benefited from the cooperation of staff at the World Bank—in particular, José Sokol and Yoon-Bo Shim—and of the staff at the IDB, especially R. Fletcher, C. Skeete, and the executive director for the Caribbean, J. Siewrattan.

My colleagues on the MDB project team, Nihal Kappagoda and Diana Tussie, who have written studies on the Asian

Development Bank and the Inter-American Development Bank, shared their knowledge and provided encouragement and comments. I have benefited from the guidance and suggestions of members of the advisory board, in particular John Lewis, Jean Quesnel, and Catherine Gwin, and of the participants of the two roundtables held in Ottawa in 1992 and 1993. I am also most grateful to Andrew Clark and Sarah Matthews at the North-South Institute for their administrative support and to Clyde Sanger and Maureen Johnson, who edited and greatly improved my text.

Chandra Hardy
Washington, D.C.

Acronyms

ACB	Agricultural Credit Bank
ACP	advisory council to the president (of the CDB)
AFI	approved financial institution
BHN	basic human needs
BMC	borrowing member country
BNTF	Basic Needs Trust Fund
BSIL	Barbados Sugar Industries Limited
CARIBCAN	Caribbean-Canada preferential tariff agreement
CARICOM	Caribbean Community and Common Market
CARIFTA	Caribbean Free Trade Association
CBI	Caribbean Basin Initiative
CDB	Caribbean Development Bank
CDC	Commonwealth Development Corporation
CDF	Caribbean Development Facility
CGCED	Caribbean Group for Cooperation in Economic Development
CIDA	Canadian International Development Agency
CTCS	Caribbean Technological Consultancy Services Network
DFC	development finance company
ECCB	Eastern Caribbean Central Bank
EDF	European Development Fund
EDI	Economic Development Institute (of the World Bank)
EEC	European Economic Community
EIB	European Investment Bank
ERP	Economic Recovery Program
EU	European Union
FAO	Food and Agriculture Organization
GCI	general capital increase
GDP	gross domestic product
GNP	gross national product

IDA	International Development Association
IDB	Inter-American Development Bank
IDRC	International Development Research Centre
IFF	Intermediate Financial Facility
IFI	international financial institution
ILPES	Latin American Institute of Economic and Social Planning
IMF	International Monetary Fund
LDC	less-developed country
MDB	multilateral development bank
MDC	more-developed country
NDB	national development bank
OCR	ordinary capital resources
OECD	Organisation for Economic Cooperation and Development
OECS	Organisation of Eastern Caribbean States
OSDF	other special development funds
OSF	other special funds
PAHO	Pan-American Health Organisation
PIEU	Post-Implementation and Evaluation Unit
PSIP	public sector investment program
SDF	special development funds
SDR	special drawing rights
SFR	special fund resources
SIDA	Swedish International Development Agency
TAF	Technical Assistance Fund
TW	Third Window (of World Bank)
UNDP	United Nations Development Programme
USAID	United States Agency for International Development
USDF	Unified Special Development Fund
UWI	University of the West Indies
VTF	Venezuelan Trust Fund
WHO	World Health Organisation

1

INTRODUCTION

The Caribbean Development Bank (CDB) is a subregional bank that has, over the last twenty-five years, focused its efforts on development of the Commonwealth Caribbean countries and, in particular, the seven small island states that form the Organisation of Eastern Caribbean States (OECS). It is small in size of staff (it has fewer than 200 at its headquarters in Barbados); and the average size of its project loans, at about $5 million,[1] is also small in comparison with the two development banks above it: the Inter-American Development Bank (IDB) and the World Bank. But the advantages of smallness, as well as proximity to and continuity of relations with the partner countries, are clear in the CDB's record. It offers the addition of a modest, but significant, success story to the worldwide chronicle of efforts to reduce poverty and improve skills in the less-developed countries.

The CDB has played an important role in the mobilization of resources for investment in parts of the Caribbean. The Bank began operations in 1970 with eighteen members and $25 million in paid-in capital subscriptions. By 1991, its financial resources amounted to almost $1 billion, and the membership had increased to 25. Overall, the CDB has financed only 6 percent of the public sector investment in the region, but in the countries of OECS, its share of the financing has been up to 40 percent.

When the CDB was launched, Canada and the United Kingdom each advanced U.S. $10 million (half paid-in and half callable) of the initial capital. This amounted to the maximum 40 percent shareholding allocated to nonregional members. Later, when France, Germany, and Italy became nonregional members, the Canadian and British shares were correspondingly reduced. The United States is not a member of the CDB since it is U.S. policy not to join any subregional bank, but its contributions to the special fund resources (the Bank's concessional window) meant that it has accounted for more than 11 percent of the CDB's total resources.

The CDB has assisted the development of the region through the provision of both hard and soft loans, technical assistance, and policy advice; regional members have also benefited from obtaining more than 50 percent of the value of procurement contracts. Special attention was given to the less-developed member countries, which have received 55 percent of total lending and 85 percent of technical assistance grants. This was deliberate policy, but the decision was aided by the fact that, until recently, Barbados and Trinidad had little need to borrow from the CDB. In addition there was no lending to Guyana during the 1980s due to a build-up of arrears. Jamaica is the CDB's largest single borrower (with 18 percent of net approvals), and most of the loans have been directed to the small-scale private sector through local financial intermediaries, channelling funds through the National Development Bank and the Agricultural Credit Bank of Jamaica.

Although the CDB has had a limited record of project loans to Jamaica, it is nevertheless a strong project-lending institution. Its professional staff is competent and well regarded, and its project processing is faster and less costly than that of the IDB or the World Bank. The management and staff are knowledgeable about local conditions, and they have the confidence and support of politicians, government officials, the private sector, and the technical staff executing projects. The high rate of success in the projects and programs financed is a measure of the bank's effectiveness as a development institution.

The project portfolio has emphasized lending to the public sector for infrastructure development, mainly in the transport sector. The projects to build feeder roads and extend and rehabilitate main roads, ports, and airports have shown good financial rates of return as have project loans to public utilities to increase the supply of power and to improve the availability of clean water and sewer facilities. More important, the CDB has been successful in helping public utilities in the less-developed countries (LDCs) to show an operating surplus. The projects to support the export of bananas and other crops in countries such as Belize and St. Lucia have also been successful, but livestock and fisheries projects have encountered financial and managerial problems.

About one-quarter of the lending has been channelled through more than twenty development finance companies (DFCs) to small and medium-sized private sector enterprises, and considerable effort was put into strengthening these institutions. Support for the social sector has been limited to the provision of loans for low- and middle-income housing, student loans for post-secondary education, and the Basic Human Needs Program (BHN), which emphasizes small community development projects.

The scope for policy-based lending was limited because the CDB has not had the staff to carry out detailed analysis of the fiscal and trade accounts nor the resources to provide balance-of-payments assistance, but the Bank has helped to channel funds from donors in support of structural adjustment. In 1976 the CDB helped to establish the Fund for Emergency Programs and Common Services in LDCs and, in response to the widespread balance-of-payments problems of its borrowers, made proposals to the aid group in 1978 that led to the creation of the Caribbean Development Facility (CDF) and the Basic Human Needs Fund to help countries implementing stabilization programs. In 1991, with the World Bank, the CDB cofinanced the economic recovery loan to Guyana—part of the package of support accompanying the clearance of arrears and the restructuring of the economy.

Country studies and project evaluation reports indicate that the CDB has had a positive impact on the OECS countries. They regard the Bank as a key partner in their economic development, and it has provided significant benefits to Barbados, partly in attracting other international agencies to the island, and partly in supporting efforts to revitalize the sugar industry and to improve the airport (and thereby the tourist industry). Because of its close ties to the region, the CDB has had a qualitative impact on economic policies beyond the resources it has made available. One example of this is the improvement in the public finances of several OECS countries, which benefited not only from macroeconomic advice but perhaps more from the effect of the CDB's policy conditions for project financing and efficiency. In the early 1970s, many of these countries were receiving budgetary support from the United Kingdom; when this support was withdrawn, they experienced severe fiscal difficulties. Today most OECS countries register budgetary surpluses.

In addition to lending, the CDB has provided resources for training and institution-building; aid coordination and economic policy advice have become important aspects of its operations. The Bank has complemented the role of governments in setting policies and has encouraged greater cooperation among Caribbean states. Lending to promote regional cooperation has been constrained by the lack of success of regional projects during the 1970s, but the CDB has subsequently supported a number of other measures in technical assistance and higher education to strengthen economic cooperation in the Caribbean and between the Caribbean and Latin America. Colombia, Venezuela, and Mexico have provided financial resources through the CDB for regional development.

The CDB is characterized by prudent and careful management. The Bank has successfully adhered to its own conservative financial policies and continuously shown a profit. The Bank receives strong support from its member governments both in meeting their debt service obligations and capital contributions. The members have supported all the general capital increases (GCIs) since 1970, and no capital subscriptions are in arrears; some members have paid-in their subscriptions in advance. The current level of paid-in capital is 22.1 percent, which is more than twice the level of the World Bank and the IDB.

The CDB has built a solid loan portfolio, and arrears are very small. In 1992, the Bank had its first borrowing on the international capital market of U.S. $30 million; it was rated by Moody's Investor Service as triple-A due to its strong financial structure, policies that minimize risk, and the support of five triple-A members.

The Bank has been very fortunate in its presidents, who have imparted a strong sense of purpose and stability to the institution. Sir Arthur Lewis (1970–1973) laid the foundation for the Bank as a sound project-lending and financial institution. He also drew attention to the structural problems (low savings, low productivity, and overvalued exchange rates) that have long constrained the region's economic growth. William Demas (1974–1988) guided the Bank through a period of steady expansion up to the early 1980s and the subsequent period of austerity for the borrowers and the Bank. During his tenure, he emphasized the need for increasing food production, improving the operations of the DFCs, supporting regional projects, and coordinating aid and national development strategies. Sir Neville Nichols (1988–present) has seen the CDB through a difficult transition period, with the departure of four senior officials and several project analysts and economists in 1988–1989. He also inherited the problem of widespread arrears on CDB loans, which the Bank addressed by refusing to approve new loans (or disburse existing ones) until arrears were cleared. This firm tactic was generally successful and led to the gradual easing of the constraints on lending. The resolution of Guyana's arrears problem in 1990 and the general capital increase in 1991 have put the CDB in a strong position for future growth.

The CDB has collaborated with the World Bank and the IDB in promoting the development of the region. Many LDCs lack direct access to funds from the larger multilateral development banks (MDBs), which find it uneconomic to process small projects. To fill this gap, the CDB has cofinanced projects with both the World Bank and the IDB and has borrowed $97 million from the World Bank and International Development Association (IDA) for on-lending, mainly to the OECS countries. The region has clearly benefited from the presence of the World Bank, the IMF, the IDB, and the CDB, who are all members of the aid group, but their effectiveness would be greatly enhanced by more collaboration in their operational and economic work.

The success of the CDB shows that there is a benefit to pluralism in the system of resource transfers. The overwhelming advantage of small, highly focused, subregional development banks like the CDB is the ability to make good project loans. The borrowers are actively involved during project preparation, and the CDB staff, who know the macroeconomic and sectoral constraints, can focus on building institutional capacity and improved project management. The CDB has a distinct advantage over the larger MDBs in the lower cost of appraisal and supervision of projects, in knowledge of the region, and in flexibility. It is also an efficient vehicle for pooling bilateral aid in support of regional programs such as basic needs, training, and environmental protection.

Looking to the future, one can only urge the governors and senior staff of the Caribbean Development Bank to play a more dynamic role in the region. The needs are clear. Poverty increased during the 1980s to the point where malnutrition was the principal cause of death among infants in Guyana and the formerly oil-rich Trinidad. Education standards fell due to budget cuts and a shortage of qualified teachers: figures for Jamaica indicate that 30 percent of primary school leavers are functionally illiterate, while half the graduates and skilled workers emigrate. With more young people reaching working age, the region needs high rates of gross domestic product (GDP) growth to keep unemployment from rising above alarming 20 to 30 percent levels. Such growth in turn requires large-scale investment and a steady increase in net capital flows, yet aid flows to the region have been declining.

In these circumstances, the CDB cannot be complacent about its record nor satisfied with the niche it has carved for itself in project lending for relatively small projects. In terms of total assets, compared with the IDB, the Bank is still a tiny organization and needs to expand its capital base. This will allow it to support larger projects, including regional projects, and reduce its operational costs. To expand its base will probably involve an increase in membership, as well as regular capital increases.

In considering future relationships, and division of responsibilities, with the World Bank and the IDB, there is clearly scope— if not an evident need—for the CDB to expand its work. This is particularly the case for the OECS countries, which are not eligible for concessionary credits from the International Development Association (IDA) "soft window" of the Bank because their per capita incomes are above the IDA ceiling, and yet they are not sufficiently creditworthy for IBRD loans. In twenty years the CDB has received $96.6 million in loans from the World Bank group and has "blended" some of these funds for on-lending to OECS countries. The CDB should become a greater channel of World Bank funds to these countries and to the region generally. Equally, IDB-CDB relationships need to be sorted out, one problem being that only five Caribbean Community and Common Market (CARICOM) countries are members of the IDB.

Beyond the mobilization of greater resources and the expansion of lending programs, the CDB should consider a more active role in two or three areas needing well-informed initiatives. One is the task of strengthening regional institutions in the face of the formation of trading blocs elsewhere, and it will require a good deal of economic analysis, coordinated with work done at the IDB and World Bank. Another is to stem some appalling damage to the environment. The CDB does not have the resources to finance, in particular, better waste management practices; but it should take the lead in spreading information about environmental problems and in helping to establish regional policies to deal with them.

Adding such responsibilities will require some relaxation of budget constraints, for the CDB needs to recruit more specialists and strengthen its economic and analytical skills. At the same time, the Bank should not disperse its efforts in undertaking too many responsibilities for economic work or in diversifying its lending beyond the areas where it has built experience and achieved success. However, it needs to show more boldness and confidence as the major advocate for the development of this region.

Note

1. Dollar figures throughout the text refer to current U.S. dollars.

PART 1

HISTORICAL SETTING AND
RECORD OF PERFORMANCE

2

A BRIEF HISTORY OF THE BANK

Institutional Framework

Origins

The Federation of the West Indies was formed in 1958 but was dissolved four years later, after Jamaica and Trinidad left to become independent states. A subsequent effort at forming a union of the "Little Eight" (Barbados, the four Windward, and the three Leeward Islands) was unsuccessful, and in July 1966 a team of experts was appointed by the United Kingdom, Canada, and the United States to carry out a survey and make recommendations for the economic development of the group. The team's recommendations included the establishment of a regional development bank. Later that year, at a conference of the sponsors of the survey and representatives of the eight countries, it was agreed that the scope of the bank should be extended to serve all the countries of the Commonwealth Caribbean.

The United Nations Development Programme (UNDP) was asked to undertake a feasibility study. In July 1967, the UNDP team submitted its report, recommending the establishment of the Caribbean Development Bank (CDB) with an initial capital of U.S. $50 million. The mission noted the enthusiasm of the region's leaders for the Bank and their willingness to contribute 1 percent of national income as capital subscription. The breakup of the West Indies Federation had been a disappointment, but it had not dampened the search for stronger regional ties. In October 1967, the heads of government of the Commonwealth Caribbean passed three resolutions supporting regional integration through the establishment of the CDB, the Caribbean Free Trade Association (CARIFTA), and the development of regional air and sea communications.

The draft agreement establishing the CDB was prepared early in 1968 and adopted in October 1969 after three ministerial meetings. In his opening remarks to the March 1968 ministerial meeting, the then prime minister of Guyana, Forbes Burnham, voiced the region's hope that the CDB could "be the institution for further bringing together the peoples of the Caribbean, and providing the structure which will finance development in the region and aid in achieving the integration of our islands and territories. If this were not the objective, if the CDB were to be but another international financial institution fortuitously, though perhaps conveniently, situated in the Caribbean, I would say that our efforts and our time have been ill-used and ill-spent." He added that there was a general commitment to the concept of a CDB "as an important piece of the machinery in the pursuit of the integration of the Caribbean."

The momentum to establish the Bank was interrupted by Jamaica's decision, in May 1968, not to participate as a member after a majority of the ministers had voted to locate the Bank in Barbados. Fortunately, this position was reversed, and Jamaica rejoined when the group met in July 1969 to set up a preparatory committee. The UNDP, the World Bank, and the Inter-American Development Bank (IDB) provided assistance to the preparatory committee, and the agreement establishing the CDB was signed in Jamaica in October 1969 and became effective in January 1970.

Purpose and Functions

Article 1 of the Charter states that the purpose of the CDB is to "contribute to the harmonious economic growth and development of the member countries in the Caribbean and to promote economic cooperation and integration among them, having special and urgent regard to the needs of the less-developed members of the region."

The main functions of the CDB are outlined in Article 2 of the Charter as follows:

a. to assist regional members in the coordination of their development programs to achieve better utilization of their resources, to make their economies more complementary, and to promote the orderly expansion of trade, in particular, intraregional trade;
b. to mobilize additional financial resources for development from within and outside the region;

c. to finance projects and programs that contribute to the development of the region or any of the members;
d. to provide appropriate technical assistance to undertake preinvestment surveys and to assist in the identification and preparation of project proposals;
e. to promote private and public investment;
f. to promote regional and local financial institutions and a regional market for credit and savings; and
g. to stimulate and encourage the development of capital markets within the region.

The CDB's purpose and functions are similar to those of the larger multilateral development banks. Its specific characteristics reflect its size and regional considerations, such as the mandate to pay special attention to the needs of the smaller and less-developed member countries and capital market development.

Membership

In 1970, there were sixteen regional and two nonregional members. Currently the membership stands at twenty-five, of which twenty are regional and five are nonregional. The following states and territories are members of the Bank:

1. Regional Commonwealth Caribbean and borrowing members: Anguilla, Antigua and Barbuda, Bahamas, Barbados, Belize, British Virgin Islands, Cayman Islands, Dominica, Grenada, Guyana, Jamaica, Montserrat, St. Kitts-Nevis, St. Lucia, St. Vincent and the Grenadines, Trinidad and Tobago, Turks and Caicos Islands.
2. Other regional: Venezuela and Colombia were admitted as regional members in 1973 and 1974 respectively. Mexico was admitted in 1982.
3. Nonregional: Canada and the United Kingdom were founding members; France became a member in 1984; Italy in 1988; and Germany in 1989. The United States supported the establishment of the CDB but was unwilling to take up membership in a subregional bank.

Only regional members can borrow from the CDB. The three regional members that are not members of the Commonwealth Caribbean may borrow only up to the amount that each has contributed in hard currency to the share capital, but they have so far chosen not to exercise the right to borrow. In other respects, the five nonregional and the three Latin American members give a multilateral character to the bank, and their guidance and support have been important to its development.

There is considerable diversity among the borrowing member countries (BMCs) in terms of size, resource endowment, and average incomes. The smallest is Anguilla, an island of 91 square kilometers; and the largest is Guyana with a land area of 215,000 square kilometers. Populations range from 7,000 for Anguilla to 2.5 million for Jamaica. Per capita incomes in 1990 ranged from $330 in Guyana to $18,300 in the Cayman Islands. In 1970 the members of CARICOM and the CDB's borrowing member countries were divided into two groups: more-developed countries (MDCs), which included the Bahamas, Barbados, Guyana, Jamaica, and Trinidad and Tobago, and the less-developed countries (LDCs), which included all the other BMCs. This division is less meaningful now as several LDCs have experienced rapid rates of economic growth over the past two decades, while some MDCs have experienced the reverse; however, given its widespread usage, these categories are maintained throughout the text.

Capital Structure and Voting Rights

The CDB started operations in 1970 with an authorized and subscribed capital of $50 million consisting of 10,000 shares, each with a face value of U.S. $5,000; half of the capital was paid-in and the rest was callable. In 1992, the CDB had an authorized capital of 115,000 shares and was capitalized at $648 million, of which $143 million (22 percent) was paid-in and $505 million was callable. The Charter stipulates that not less than 60 percent of the authorized share capital should be held by the regional members; in 1992, regional members held 60.34 percent of the subscribed capital. Jamaica and Trinidad and Tobago are the largest shareholders with each holding 16.63 percent of the total shares. The Bahamas hold 4.91 percent; Guyana, 3.58 percent; and Barbados, 3.12 percent. Colombia, Mexico, and Venezuela each hold 3.13 percent. Canada and the United Kingdom started with 20 percent of the shares, each and now hold 10.44 percent each. France, Germany, and Italy hold 6.26 percent each.

Regional members also have a built-in majority in terms of voting rights, because the Articles of Agreement allow each member 150 votes plus one additional vote for each share of capital stock held; in 1992, regional members held 61.05 percent of the voting rights. At a special meeting in 1971, the Board of Governors decided that Commonwealth Caribbean members should always have a majority of the voting power and a majority of the directors. Although ownership and control of the CDB rests with the regional members, Board decisions are reached by consensus and the relationship between regional and nonregional members has always been harmonious, a fortuitous circumstance because the bank depends heavily on outside sources for its funding. At the end of 1992, nonregional members provided 34.6 percent of the CDB's total resources, which amounted to U.S. $984.7 million. Regional members accounted for 21.5 percent, with Commonwealth Caribbean members accounting for 11.9 percent; nonmember countries provided 14.8 percent, including 11.5 percent from the United States and a total of 3.3 percent from the Netherlands, Nigeria, and Sweden; 15 percent came from the multilateral financial institutions and the international capital market; and 14 percent was accumulated net income and miscellaneous revenue.

Organization and Management

The governing board.   Each member country is represented on the CDB's Board of Governors by a governor and an alternate, except for Anguilla, the British Virgin Islands, Cayman Islands, Montserrat, and the Turks and Caicos Islands, which jointly elect one governor. The governing board meets at least once a year. The governors delegate some of their responsibility to the nonresident Board of Directors comprising seventeen members (twelve regional and five nonregional), which normally meets about six times a year. The directors are appointed for renewable two-year periods, and they are responsible for setting general policy and directing the bank's operations, including loan and investment approvals. The CDB president is the chairman of the Board of Directors.

The Bank's accountability to the governing board is maintained through the review of internal and external audits. Internal audit and postimplementation evaluations are performed by staff units reporting directly to the president. External audits have been carried out by Price Waterhouse since the bank's inception. None of their audit reports has ever been qualified.

The president.   The CDB has had three presidents over the past twenty years—Sir Arthur Lewis (1970–1973), William Demas (1974–1988), and Sir Neville Nichols (1988–present)—and each has placed a strong and continuing imprint on the institution. The respect accorded to the CDB from its earliest days rested on the reputation of Sir Arthur Lewis—as an economist, university professor, author, statesman, and vice-chancellor of the University of the West Indies (UWI). A tall, somewhat shy and reticent man, he was a tireless and meticulous worker who gave stature and intellectual and personal integrity to the bank. Sir Arthur is credited with ensuring that the CDB would be insulated from political interference by the region's governments. Article 35 of the Charter and the 1970 resolution of the Board of Governors affirmed that the Board of Directors would only consider for approval projects that had been appraised and presented by the Bank's staff.

Sir Arthur's clear and succinct analysis of the region's economic problems in his 1972 annual meeting speech is still valid today. He noted the heavy concentration on the export of primary commodities, the pressure on wages to rise faster than productivity, the overvaluation of exchange rates, and the enormous task of alleviating poverty and providing jobs. However, he was optimistic about the prospects of the region if appropriate economic policies were adopted. He was a lifelong proponent of economic and political union in the region, and his speech accepting the Nobel Prize for Economics in 1979 was a strong argument for increased economic cooperation among developing countries.[1] Sir Arthur also ensured that the debate about whether the CDB was a bank or a development institution would become a nonissue. He said that the Bank had to be a solid financial institution if it was to have any developmental function, and this required the adoption of sound procedures in the identification, appraisal, and supervision of projects and adherence to prudent financial policies.

Under President Demas, the CDB continued to develop its project-lending capability and to provide economic and technical support to its borrowers while looking for ways to mobilize concessional funds for balance-of-payments support and poverty alleviation. The years 1974–1982 coincided with a series of global shocks that created enormous hardships in the region. The CDB was successful in mobilizing resources for lending from Trinidad and Tobago, regional central banks, and Venezuela and in establishing a fund to finance emergency programs and common services in the LDCs. Contributions to the fund came from the more-developed member countries and the United Kingdom.

Under the leadership of President Demas, cumulative net loan approvals expanded from $35 million in 1974 to $392 million in 1982; lending tripled through the development finance companies

(DFCs), which served to channel CDB funds to smaller enterprises. Several projects were approved to support regional integration. In addition to lending, the CDB expanded its development agency functions beyond the provision of technical assistance and training to include aid coordination and economic policy advice. The years 1983–1987 saw increased emphasis on stabilization and adjustment in the borrowing countries and a marked decline in lending; this resulted from the payment difficulties of some borrowers and the bank's own resource constraints.

Sir Neville Nichols joined the CDB's staff in 1971 as legal counsel; he held several senior management positions before becoming president in 1988. He guided the bank through a difficult period following the departure in 1988 of four senior officers—the president, vice-president (corporate services), director of projects, and senior manager (agriculture and industry division). The constraint on lending was lifted with the expansion of membership in 1988 and 1989, the clearance of Guyana's arrears in 1990, and the general capital increase in 1991. Under Sir Neville's leadership, the CDB has steadily expanded the volume of operations and the quality of its output, and in May 1993, he was elected to a second five-year term.

Staffing. The present organizational structure is the result of the 1984–1985 restructuring that was designed to improve efficiency and accountability. The legal, finance, and administration departments were placed under the vice-president of corporate services, and the projects and economics departments were placed under the vice-president of operations. The senior management team consists of two vice-presidents and four department directors who are all members of the advisory council to the president (ACP), which is the most important committee within the CDB. The ACP meets weekly to discuss issues requiring decisions by management.

There has been a steady reduction in the size of the staff since 1981—from 219 to the current level of 188, of which eighty-eight are professional positions and 100 are support staff. Apart from the turnover of senior staff noted earlier and the departure of three economists who left to join the World Bank and the International Monetary Fund (IMF) in 1988, most of the staff have been with the Bank for more than ten years. The quality of the professional staff is considered high by colleagues in the World Bank and IDB and by the borrowers, but some of the problems of morale and underutilization of skills that are usually associated with small-scale operations, diversified responsibilities, and a flat organizational structure were evident.

A number of measures were taken during the 1980s to increase the efficiency of Bank operations, including an Organization and Management Productivity Study in 1985. The study's objective was to reduce the time spent on administration and ensure that staff resources were directed mainly to projects and economic work. In the 1990 follow-up study, the researchers looked for ways to cut high-cost and unessential activities. They found that staff members had as many as twenty to forty different tasks to perform, which is not unusual in small organizations, and that, as the study stated, "specialization is precluded by the fragmentation of staff."

Another conclusion of the study was that "some increase in the number, the quality and skill-mix of the staff is imperative for achieving the level of growth and performance expected in the 1990s." As the scope of the Bank's activities expands, the squeeze on manpower resources is becoming severe. Staff often cannot be released for training because this could delay loan operations or economic work. Flexibility in assignments is also limited—when staff are released to carry out special assignments, such as assistance to CARICOM on the implementation of the Common External Tariff (CET), or on the privatization of the regional airline Leeward Islands Air Transport, or to IDB for a study of the constraints to private sector lending—their regular work has to be shared by their colleagues. Technical staff need to broaden their skills and keep abreast of developments in their field. However, the CDB has only one power engineer and one water engineer, each appraising up to four projects a year in addition to supervising a large project portfolio, and there are no staff to spare for training or secondment.

Despite the constraints, no major staff increases are currently anticipated. Efforts are being made to develop existing staff resources through training, and staff are being encouraged to become more multiskilled. A number of options are under consideration for more effective staff utilization; these include the use of technical assistance grants to engage consultants for project preparation and supervision; recruitment of specialists for short-term assignments; removal of the boundaries between units so that staff can be easily reassigned to where they are needed; and combining economic and project identification missions so that staff can visit BMCs as a team.

Studies are also continuing on the improvement of technical

support, internal information systems, and the provision of secretarial services. The highest outlay on a single type of activity identified in the 1990 productivity study was secretarial services employed to type appraisal reports. The wider availability of personal computers to professional staff and the standardization of appraisal reports would greatly reduce the need for secretarial services. Most of the existing support staff could then be trained at a modest cost to take over some of the necessary but routine tasks that are carried out by the professional staff.

There are many advantages to the CDB's small size, such as a sense of cohesiveness and the familiarity of the staff with what has worked well elsewhere. There are, however, several disadvantages including the limits on professional specialization and upward mobility. To be effective, the CDB's staff must remain small, highly skilled and flexible; to achieve this a more innovative program of career development, mobility, staff training, and motivation is needed. Greater consideration should be given to internal reassignment and short-term secondment to the IDB and the World Bank to broaden staff skills and experience. Staff not fully utilized due to shifts in the lending program's composition or staff who have been in one assignment for a long time should be exposed to work in other areas of the bank or sent abroad on assignment. Staff who have been seconded to borrowing countries describe these assignments as their best, and professionally most rewarding, experience. The CDB could be reimbursed by UNDP or other agencies for these assignments, and it could then hire consultants for needed short-term jobs.

Bank Operations: Policies and Procedures

The Charter requires the CDB to adhere to sound development banking principles and to finance only economically sound, technically feasible, and properly appraised projects in the private and public sectors through debt or equity investments. Its operational policies and procedures are described in a manual that specifies that projects financed from its ordinary capital resources (OCR) on conventional terms must have financial and economic rates of return not lower than the opportunity cost of capital, and that projects financed on concessional terms from special fund resources (SFR) must have high economic rates of return. All borrowing members are eligible to receive concessional loans, but, traditionally, these funds have gone mainly to the LDCs.

The CDB finances the foreign exchange costs of projects and, to a limited extent, local currency expenditures. Borrowers are required to make an appropriate contribution to the cost of the project. The CDB can finance up to 80 percent of project costs in LDCs (70 percent in MDCs) on OCR loans and up to 90 percent of project costs on special fund operations (80 percent in MDCs). Loans to private borrowers are limited to two-thirds of the project cost and must carry satisfactory security. The minimum size of a loan is $200,000, but few loans are now made for less than $1 million; smaller projects are generally financed from CDB loans to the development finance companies.

Lending Terms

The OCR lending rate, which is variable, is set to yield a rate of return of 7 percent per annum on the CDB's usable capital. The current lending rate is 7.5 percent to the public sector and private sector financial intermediaries, and 9.5 percent on direct loans to the private sector. Loan repayments are made in the currency loaned, and the exchange risk is carried by the borrower. The maturity of OCR loans is determined on project grounds and generally is thirteen to twenty-three years with three to five years' grace. SFR loan terms range from 2 percent per annum for forty years including ten years' grace, to 5 percent per annum for up to twenty years including five years' grace depending on the country conditions. CDB's lending terms and conditions are summarized in Table A1 in the Appendix.

Project Appraisal

The CDB is primarily a project-lending institution, and project identification, appraisal, and supervision are carried out according to established procedures. The staff spend a lot of time on project identification and preparation; following preparation, projects are appraised quickly, and reports are generally written within two months. Project appraisals are of a high standard in comparison with those of the larger MDBs, and efforts are being made to give increased attention in appraisal reports to sectoral issues, environmental impact, and institution building. Collaboration between World Bank and CDB staff to improve appraisal techniques for transport projects has been very successful; the CDB is now preparing, with the help of consultants, a project information system that will improve project analysis further.

After review at the divisional and departmental level, appraisal reports are sent to the loan committee, which is chaired by the vice-president of operations. The CDB is proud of its success in reducing the cost and the time in moving projects from identification to approval, and it has developed a considerable advantage as a financial intermediary due to its low project-processing cost. Rough estimates per project have been calculated at $200,000 for the CDB, $750,000 for the IDB, and $1 million for the World Bank. No two projects are identical, therefore these estimates can only be considered indicative, but they support other data that suggest that the CDB's project-processing costs are four to five times lower than those of the IDB and the World Bank.

Supervision is intensive during the period of project implementation, and, unlike other MDBs, the CDB maintains supervision after project completion. The Post-Implementation and Evaluation Unit (PIEU) has prepared monitoring indicators for inclusion in appraisal reports to facilitate supervision. Management pays close attention to the progress of project implementation and the pace of disbursement, but the shortage of experienced financial analysts and economists limits the CDB's ability to monitor other aspects of performance, such as operating efficiency and institutional development.

Procurement policies and disbursement procedures on OCR loans are similar to those of other MDBs. International competitive bidding is required on projects of over $750,000 and qualified bids are allowed for smaller contracts. Similarly, procurement for SFR-funded projects is limited to member countries and to those countries contributing to SFR.[2]

Financial Policies

The CDB offers two types of financing: (1) operations financed on conventional terms from OCR and at the CDB's own risk exclusively, and (2) operations financed on concessionary terms from SFR by way of special development funds and trust funds provided by members, nonmembers, and donor agencies. OCR operations accounted for 43 percent of total financing approvals, and SFR operations accounted for 57 percent at the end of 1992. This blend of resources available through the CDB makes it unique among the multilateral development banks in the overall degree of concessionality of its lending.

In making loans, the CDB is required by its Charter to consider the creditworthiness of the borrower, and, once an investment is made, the bank must ensure that the funds are used with economy and efficiency. In 1987, the CDB adopted revised financial policies and operating guidelines for the management of its OCR that, among other provisions, call for:

a. maintenance of an interest coverage ratio (ICR)[3] of not less than 1.75 times;
b. restricting OCR lending to the sum of net paid-in capital, ordinary reserves, and the callable capital of members of the Organisation for Economic Cooperation and Development (OECD);
c. OCR borrowing not to exceed the callable capital of OECD countries, exposure not to exceed 50 percent of equity in any country, no new loans to countries in arrears, suspension of disbursements after four months in arrears, and provisioning against nonperforming loans;
d. a minimum reserves-to-loans ratio of 30 percent;
e. loans outstanding to the largest debtor not to exceed ordinary reserves; and
f. loans outstanding to the three largest borrowers not to exceed total capital.

The CDB began the 1990s in a strong financial position and is well placed to play a larger role in the development of the region. The target financial ratios set in 1987 have been achieved, a general capital increase of $200 million was approved in January 1991, and negotiations were completed in 1991 for the replenishment of the special development fund (SDF) at $124 million for 1992–1995. In 1990, the CDB worked closely with the World Bank, the IMF, and bilateral donors on the Economic Recovery Program (ERP) for Guyana; this resulted in the clearance of Guyana's arrears and the largest loan ($42 million) in the bank's history. (See Table 2.1.)

Notes

1. W. Arthur Lewis, "The Slowing Down of the Engine of Growth," *American Economic Review* 70, no. 4, September 1980: 555–564.
2. *Guidelines for Procurement*, CDB, October 1992.
3. The interest coverage ratio is defined as net income before deducting the total interest expenses on borrowings, divided by the total interest expenses on borrowings. The ICR is used to measure the likelihood that interest payments could be threatened by a decline in net income.

Table 2.1   Financial Resources: 1992 (in millions of dollars)

	OCR	SFR[a]	Total	Percent
Paid-up capital	143.4		143.4	10.7
Callable capital[b]	410.2		410.2	30.7
Technical assistance		70.1	70.1	5.2
Grants				
Caribbean members		35.2	35.2	2.6
Other regional members		52.1	52.1	3.9
Nonregional members		259.5	259.5	19.4
Nonmembers		52.5	52.5	3.9
Concessionary loans				
Caribbean members		1.5	1.5	0.1
Nonregional members		13.6	13.6	1.0
Nonmembers		136.1	136.1	10.2
Reserves	97.7	65.4	163.1	12.2
Total	651.3	686.0	1,337.3	100.0

Source: CDB.
Notes: a. Includes SDF and other special fund resources.
b. Net of borrowing.

3

Borrowing Country Experience

The Regional Economy

The Commonwealth Caribbean consists of twelve independent countries (Antigua and Barbuda, the Bahamas, Barbados, Belize, Dominica, Grenada, Guyana, Jamaica, St. Lucia, St. Vincent and the Grenadines, St. Kitts-Nevis, and Trinidad and Tobago), and five U.K. dependencies (Anguilla, British Virgin Islands, Cayman Islands, Montserrat, and the Turks and Caicos Islands). The total population of the region is 5.7 million, and it has been growing at 1.3 percent per annum. Regional gross national product (GNP) is about $10 billion, and the average per capita income is $3,000, which puts all the countries in the category of middle- or upper-income developing countries except low-income Guyana (see Table A2).

Progress has also been made in raising living standards through improved access to education, preventive health care, improved water supply, and sanitation. The infant mortality rate is less than 20 per 1,000, and life expectancy has risen to seventy-one years. Literacy rates are over 90 percent in most countries, and enrollment in primary and secondary schools has steadily expanded. The distribution of the benefits of growth has been uneven, however, and large pockets of poverty exist throughout the region. Unemployment rates range from 10 to 35 percent and are highest among women and young people. Emigration has traditionally provided a safety valve for chronically high rates of unemployment, but the steady exodus of professionals has reduced the skill-mix of the remaining labor force and has adversely affected both the quality and the provision of education and primary health care services.

Throughout the region, the structure of output is concentrated in a few sectors. Services account for 50–65 percent of total output. This includes tourism (a major industry in the OECS, the dependencies, the Bahamas, Barbados, and Jamaica), construction, the public sector, and wholesale and retail trade. The share of agriculture has been falling throughout the region and accounts for less than 10 percent of gross domestic product (GDP) except in land-rich Belize and Guyana. The share of manufacturing in GDP varies from 5 percent in the smaller islands to 20 percent in Jamaica and Barbados; output in the sector is constrained by high production costs and heavy reliance on imported materials. Mining is an important source of public revenue in Guyana, Jamaica, and Trinidad and Tobago but provides little employment.

The region is characterized by small, open economies, highly vulnerable to fluctuations in the international economy. It is equally vulnerable to hurricanes and the unpredictable damage they wreak. External trade accounts for more than 100 percent of GDP in most countries; exports are limited to a few primary commodities (sugar, bananas, and bauxite) facing low-income and price elasticities, and imports consist of food and manufactured goods. Sugar accounts for between 27–39 percent of the merchandise exports of Belize, Guyana, and St. Kitts-Nevis, while bananas account for 22–82 percent of the merchandise exports of Dominica, Grenada, St. Lucia, and St. Vincent and the Grenadines. Both crops are produced at costs above world market prices and depend on preferential access to U.S. and European markets. In the OECS countries, food accounts for 21–35 percent of total imports; in Guyana, Barbados, Trinidad and Tobago, and Jamaica, the ratio varies between 15 and 20 percent.

The bulk of the region's trade is with the industrial countries. Intraregional trade accounts for around 10 percent of total trade, and, after expanding rapidly in the 1970s, intraregional trade declined steadily during the 1980s. Manufacturing accounts for one-half and agriculture for one-third of intraregional exports. Regional trade has been more dynamic in the OECS countries, where intraregional exports account for nearly half of total merchandise exports. Over the past decade, the contraction in demand in the MDCs, trade and payments restrictions, and the suspension of the CARICOM Multilateral Clearing Facility in 1983 have contributed to the decline in intraregional trade.

The region is dependent on large inflows of foreign capital to finance investment. National savings rates have hovered around 10 to 12 percent of GDP, while investment rates have averaged 24 percent of GDP. Public savings rates are low because the tax base is limited, and revenues do not match large public sector expenditures on social services, which account for 40 percent of total expenditures, investment in infrastructure, and public sector employment. Financial markets in the region generally consist of a central bank, national development banks, commercial banks that are largely foreign-owned, and insurance companies. Jamaica, Barbados, and Trinidad have made progress in capital market development, but the limited size of the market increases transaction costs.

The 1970s produced a period of severe difficulties for the Caribbean region. In 1971, the depreciation of the U.S. dollar and the collapse of the Bretton Woods system of fixed exchange rates ushered in an era of fluctuating currency and interest rates. The quadrupling of oil prices in 1973 resulted in large imbalances in global payments, and this set off another round of inflation and instability in interest and exchange rates. There was a slight recovery in the industrial countries in 1976 and 1978, but GDP growth slowed again after the second oil shock in 1979. These events contributed to a sharp drop in agricultural and manufacturing output and tourism in the region. Rising import prices resulted in heavy losses in terms of trade and in growing payments imbalances in all the countries except Trinidad and Tobago, an oil exporter. In the late 1970s, Guyana and Jamaica entered into stabilization programs with the IMF; however, by the decade's end, both countries had terminated their programs and had begun to accumulate sizeable arrears.

In the early 1980s, it became clear that the MDCs would have to undertake more stringent stabilization and adjustment measures because the recovery in the industrial countries was not resulting in growth and recovery in MDC economies. Lower export prices for oil caused significant output and income losses to Trinidad and Tobago; public sector employees were hurt by wage and salary cuts; and unemployment among young people doubled. Despite a number of improvements in policy and heavy external borrowing, Jamaica continued to experience slow growth and payment difficulties. Barbados experienced an erosion of its competitiveness; and Guyana was burdened by high debt, unfavorable terms of trade, and economic mismanagement. For most of the decade, real per capita GDP growth rates were negative for Guyana, Jamaica, and Trinidad and Tobago, while Barbados recorded only marginal gains. By contrast, the LDCs registered significant gains in per capita income during the 1980s. These countries were, to a large extent, insulated from the international crises of the 1970s because their economies were less developed and had fewer linkages with the international economy. They grew rapidly during the 1980s because they were able to benefit from the recovery of tourism, increased capital inflows, preferential markets for their exports, and good economic management.

The Caribbean Group for Cooperation in Economic Development (CGCED) was established in 1978 to coordinate the flow of financial and technical support for the region. The World Bank chairs this group of traditional donors and newer sources of funding. Its creation—and mightiest effort—was prompted by the distressful situation in Jamaica, but it has also reviewed policies of all CDB regional members, as well as those of Haiti and the Dominican Republic. Under the aegis of the CGCED, net capital inflows to the region climbed steadily from $430 million in 1978 to $1,089 million in 1982 (see Table 3.1). The largest increase was from bilateral sources, but both multilateral and private flows also increased during this period. After the debt crisis struck in 1982, net capital flows fell sharply to $324 million in 1987, precipitated by a decline in official flows and the withdrawal of commercial bank lending. The share of private sector flows in total net flows declined from 13 percent in 1982 to -43 percent in 1990.

The total debt of the region was $12 billion in 1992 and in the

Table 3.1   Net Capital Flows to CARICOM Members (in millions of dollars)

	1978	1982	1987	1990
Antigua and Barbuda	2.0	10.8	60.2	na
Bahamas	13.0[a]	68.0	−29.2	0
Barbados	19.0	82.4	−27.7	0
Belize	17.0	17.1	20.0	21.4
Dominica	6.0	16.0	8.0	13.8
Grenada	3.0	13.9	20.7	22.4
Guyana	51.0	109.1	215.1	165.6
Jamaica	190.0	606.0	120.4	58.4
St. Kitts-Nevis	2.0	3.7	11.5	7.8
St. Lucia	2.0	7.2	15.7	10.0
St. Vincent and the Grenadines	5.0	8.1	13.5	11.4
Trinidad and Tobago	117.0	132.8	−125.2	−4.0
Total	430.0	1,089.0	323.7	329.2

Source: World Bank.

heavily indebted countries—Jamaica, Guyana, Antigua and Barbuda, and Grenada—high debt service has become the principal obstacle to increasing net flows. The Brady Plan provided some relief for middle-income countries heavily indebted to commercial banks, but the debt problem in the Caribbean relates mainly to official debt. Debt service payments account for 40–50 percent of export earnings; net transfers (net inflows less interest payments) were negative at about $100 million per annum between 1984 and 1986, and between 1987 and 1989 net transfers out of the region totalled $1 billion. Negative net transfers mostly affected the MDCs, while most of the OECS countries continued to enjoy positive transfers.

The recession in the industrial countries contributes to the slowdown of growth in the region. The terms of trade worsened in 1989–1992, and payments imbalances remain large; all of the countries in the region are implementing stabilization and adjustment programs aimed at reducing deficits, increasing the efficiency of resource use, and giving a larger role to the private sector. A few are showing signs of a modest recovery. In Jamaica and Trinidad and Tobago, real GDP growth has been positive but low; in Guyana, the pace of GDP growth has picked up after more than a decade of decline.

Prospects for Growth by Sector

All of the CDB's borrowers face difficult problems in the coming decade and must make major adjustments to restructure their economies, improve productivity, and introduce innovations to accelerate GDP growth. Governments are giving increased priority to agricultural diversification, the search for new exports and markets, and measures to alleviate poverty and protect the environment.

Agriculture remains a major source of foreign exchange, income, and employment for about 25 percent of the labor force, although the area under cultivation has declined. One of the constraints to increased production is the distribution of farmland; this is skewed in favor of a few large producers, leaving most small farmers with plots of an uneconomic size. The result is rural migration, inadequate capital investment in the sector, and the application of backward technologies. Other constraints are widening disparities in earnings in agricultural and other sectors and illustrating weaknesses in government support services and pricing policies. High wages in other sectors put pressure on costs and contribute to agricultural labor shortages. The governments in the region recognize the need to revitalize the agricultural sector to raise rural incomes and support the balance-of-payments.

The production of sugar remains well below the levels reached in the 1970s and 1980s, especially in Guyana and St. Kitts-Nevis. The revival of the industry is hampered by growing uncertainty about the ability of the region to maintain its preferential markets and anxiety about the slow growth of world trade. Between 1982 and 1988, U.S. quotas were cut by 70 percent, and in 1990 Congress extended the protection given to U.S. growers for another five years.

There is also considerable uncertainty regarding the future of preferential trading arrangements for bananas. Almost all of the banana exports go to the United Kingdom, where they receive higher than world market prices under the Lomé Convention. Production shortfalls have resulted in unfilled quotas being met by lower-cost Central American producers, and there is considerable apprehension in the Windward Islands where bananas account for 55 percent of export earnings. The recent decision by the European Union (EU) to establish a quota and licensing system for banana imports from Latin America allows regional producers to maintain preferential access to the U.K. market; however, this market will become more competitive as the pressure mounts for Europe to liberalize its agricultural trade. Regional producers need increased investment to raise productivity and improve the quality of their banana exports while implementing agricultural diversification programs.

Industry consists mainly of light manufacturing except in Trinidad and Tobago, Jamaica, and Guyana, which process some minerals. The MDCs account for over 90 percent of the region's manufacturing, but the sector accounts for less than 10 percent of their GDP and 12 percent of employment. The region is a high-cost producer of manufactured goods and will face increased foreign competition as trade barriers are lowered in North America and in the region. In the mining sector, bauxite production has picked up in Jamaica and Guyana, but the recession in the industrial countries will continue to depress demand and prices. The increase in petroleum prices following the Gulf War in 1991 was a welcome boost to the balance-of-payments of Trinidad and Tobago; Barbados stepped up production and was able to satisfy 40 percent of its domestic requirements in 1990; but for the oil-importing countries the increases in oil prices resulted in increases in electricity tariffs, air fares, and fuel prices.

Tourism is likely to remain the major source of growth. The number of tourists increased from 3.7 million in 1970 to 11.8 million in 1990; strong increases were registered by Anguilla, Dominica, Grenada, Jamaica, and St. Vincent and the Grenadines. However, recent data indicate a slowing down in the number of visitors and a shift in favor of cruise-ship arrivals who spend less than stopover visitors. The drop in receipts from tourism reflects the economic downturn and demographic changes in the United States and United Kingdom, competition from other markets, and a preference for cruise-ship packages. A regional strategy for the sector, improved air access, and aggressive promotion of different market segments will be needed to revive growth.

The high rate of unemployment, particularly among school-leavers, is a major social and economic problem, despite continued emigration. A large proportion of the unemployed is unskilled and unemployable. If wages do not fall, the skill-mix and productivity will need to rise; this will require increased investment in education and reform of the curriculum. Several countries are following the example of the Bahamas in developing new business in the provision of financial and data processing services. These and other knowledge-based services (legal, health, marketing, and research) hold out considerable promise for the region, but their development will require a stable political, economic, and regulatory environment and a better-trained labor force.

Continued emphasis will need to be given to macroeconomic stability. The OECS countries have pursued prudent financial policies and have a low debt burden (except for Antigua and Barbuda and Grenada). However, despite their high income levels, they are not creditworthy for conventional borrowing due to their vulnerability to natural disasters and shifts in the world economy. They will continue to rely on concessionary foreign capital inflows to finance new investments, improve productivity, and develop new exports. The MDCs face long-term structural adjustment, growing poverty, a large debt overhang, and negative net transfers. Jamaica has continuously pursued adjustment since the early 1980s, and, while these efforts have produced good results, a sustained and broad-based recovery is not yet in sight. Trinidad and Tobago and Guyana are working their way out of deep-rooted structural rigidities and imbalances, and Barbados is beginning to experience some of the socioeconomic difficulties the other countries have suffered for a long time. All the MDCs need high levels of capital inflows to support their adjustment efforts.

The financial prospects of the region are not very bright. Several borrowers are facing graduation from the International Development Association (IDA) and the World Bank, and no early increase in commercial bank lending is foreseen. This means that increased demands will be put on the CDB and the IDB to make available larger amounts of lending on concessional terms, and greater efforts will be needed to attract private investment. Over the past two decades the CDB's borrowers have shown considerable resilience and flexibility in adapting to difficult international economic conditions. There is no reason to believe that they will be any less resilient in the future, and they should continue to register rates of economic growth of 3 to 4 percent per annum in the coming decade.

4

LENDING OPERATIONS

From 1970 to 1992, the CDB's total financing approvals amounted to $1,100 million, of which 91 percent ($1,002 million) was for loans and 9 percent was for technical assistance grants; disbursements were $800 million or 73 percent of net approvals. Nearly all the lending has been for projects; the total cost of projects financed by these loans was $2.1 billion, of which the CDB provided 54 percent, borrowers 32 percent, and foreign sources 14 percent. The total investment in the region during this period was about $15 billion, with the CDB financing 7.3 percent of that total.

The CDB's largest borrower is Jamaica, accounting for 18 percent of net approvals, followed by Guyana (9 percent), St. Lucia (8 percent), Barbados, Belize and Dominica (7 percent each), and Bahamas, Grenada, and St.Vincent and the Grenadines (6 percent each); the remaining 26 percent is shared among eight members and regional projects. The LDCs have received 52 percent of net loan approvals and 73 percent of concessionary funds; they have also received 85 percent of the grant financing to support technical assistance, training, and institutional development.

Most of the lending has gone into infrastructure development and nearly 25 percent of the loans went to DFCs, which serve as intermediaries for the CDB's resources to reach small and medium-sized enterprises in agriculture, industry, and tourism and for the provision of housing and student loans. The emphasis given to developing the region's economic infrastructure reflected the relatively large per capita requirements needed to stimulate production and to promote tourism (see Table 4.1).

During the first decade, the bank gave priority to developing projects in the LDCs. Loans to the MDCs were limited because they had access to development credits from other sources and could often borrow more cheaply than from the CDB. The pro-

Table 4.1   The CDB Loan Approvals by Sector: 1970–1992 (in millions of
dollars)

	Direct	Indirect	Total	Percent
Infrastructure	407.0	42.0[a]	449.0	44.8
Agriculture[b]	39.2	86.6	125.8	12.6
Industry, mining, and tourism	176.3	92.2	268.5	26.8
Other[c]	139.8	19.1	158.9	15.8
Total	762.3	239.9	1,002.2	100.0

Source: CDB.
Notes: a. Includes mortgage finance.
b. Excludes feeder roads.
c. Includes disaster rehabilitation, education, structural adjustment, and multi-sector loans.

grams initiated during the first four years included farm improvement credit, agricultural production credit and feeder roads to support agricultural development, and the small industry credit scheme and the industrial estates program to finance the construction of factory buildings. In the social sectors, the student loan scheme, the urban working-class housing program, and mortgage financing were developed to help less well-off families.

Start-up was slow. The lack of trained professionals in the LDCs meant that the CDB had to do most of the work to identify and prepare projects, and there were major delays in disbursement because the borrowers were unfamiliar with the procedures for tendering loan proposals, procuring loans, and satisfying loan conditions. In 1973, the CDB recruited five field officers to assist borrowers in completing the formalities of signing loans and getting projects started. In the second half of the 1970s, the region was buffeted by a series of global shocks that caused enormous hardship and widening payment imbalances. Project costs escalated and domestic savings rates declined, which further increased the demand for external financing. The CDB was successful in mobilizing $50 million from regional sources for its OCR operations and in establishing the Fund for Emergency Programs and Common Services to make concessionary loans to the LDCs.

In the 1980s, the lending program grew extremely slowly due to financing difficulties of borrowers and resource shortages. The CDB made proposals to the consultative aid group that resulted in concessional resources being channelled through the CDB to support program lending to the MDCs and to establish the Basic Human Needs Trust Fund to finance small labor-intensive projects in the LDCs. Both programs were financed by the United States Agency for International Development (USAID).

Infrastructure

Infrastructure has had a prominent place in the bank's lending program, accounting for over 40 percent of total lending. Between 1970 and 1992, direct loans for infrastructure amounted to $407 million, with most of the lending going to the transport sector (71 percent) and public utilities (25.6 percent). (See Table 4.2.)

Table 4.2   Lending to Infrastructure: 1970–1992

	Millions of Dollars	Percent
Transport sector	273.6	67.3
Road transport	119.3	29.3
Sea transport	80.8	19.9
Air transport	73.5	18.1
Sea defense (drainage and land rehabilitation)	15.2	3.7
Public utilities	104.4	25.6
Power	38.6	9.5
Water supply	57.5	14.1
Communication	8.3	2.0
Housing[a]	13.8	3.4
Total	407.0	100.0

Source: CDB.
Note: a Excludes mortgage finance credits.

The feeder roads program accounted for about one-third of the loans to road transport and was designed to reduce the damage to the banana crop and to open new areas for cultivation. The cumulative volume of lending for feeder roads reached $40 million in 1992 for twenty projects, the principal borrowers being Grenada ($11.4 million), St. Vincent and the Grenadines ($9.6 million), St. Lucia ($6.5 million), Dominica ($5.5 million), and Belize ($5 million). The CDB has acquired expertise in the design of feeder roads that has contributed to improved projects, and increased attention is being given to assessing the environmental impact of opening new areas for cultivation and to the need for better road maintenance.

The emphasis on air and sea transport has improved access to export markets and facilitated the growth of tourism. In the power sector, the Bank has provided financing for investments designed to meet projected demand and end outages. Particular attention was paid to energy efficiency, institutional strengthening, and economic pricing; most of the power companies are now running profitably and can borrow on their own account for expansion. In addition to providing capital for investment, the Bank has made important contributions to institutional strengthening through the creation of statutory agencies or private companies (wholly or partly owned by the government) in the ports, water, and power sectors. In St. Lucia, the CDB helped to establish the port and airport authority to manage the country's two major modes of transport. In 1992, the agency had a surplus of $20 million that enabled it to borrow on its own account and make its own contribution to investment projects.

Infrastructure will continue to account for a major part of the lending program in the 1990s. However, emphasis will be given to improved maintenance, self-liquidating investments, the privatization of utilities, policy improvements, and environmental protection. Continued emphasis will be put on feeder roads and the rehabilitation of main roads on the condition that adequate provision is made by the borrowers for maintenance.

Large investments have gone into the construction of ports in the LDCs, and priority will be given to the rehabilitation and improvement of the existing infrastructure and the provision of technical assistance to improve operating systems and management techniques. Several borrowers are upgrading their waterfront areas to take advantage of the expansion of the cruise-ship market; others need to improve the facilities to handle the growing trend towards containerization.

Lending to the water sector will continue to be a priority. The need for improved water supplies and sewerage systems is very high, given increasing evidence of water pollution arising from chemical contamination and poor waste disposal. Emphasis will be on improving water quality and sewage disposal methods and putting the water utilities on a self-financing basis. In the power sector, the CDB will continue to provide assistance for improving and expanding power generation, incorporating where possible renewable energy sources, improving transmission and distribution networks, minimizing losses, improving conservation, and strengthening institutional foundations.

Lending for housing began in 1974 with the establishment of urban working-class settlements and the provision of primary and secondary mortgages. The CDB is currently financing housing

construction only through the primary mortgage programs channelled through the DFCs. However, plans are under consideration
to lend more for sites and services development, following a loan
in 1991 to St. Kitts-Nevis to establish a shelter infrastructure
revolving fund and a special mortgage program mainly for the
benefit of low-income families, especially those headed by
women.

Agriculture

Loans to the agricultural sector have averaged 12 percent of total
lending and have been directed towards providing credit for farm
improvements, the purchase of inputs and the establishment of
marketing outlets; encouraging new entrants to the sector through
the sale or lease of agricultural lands; promoting the development
of farming organizations; and supporting fish and livestock production. Over 1970–1992, loans to agriculture (excluding feeder
roads) totalled $130.1 million, two-thirds being channelled
through financial intermediaries (see Table 4.3).

Table 4.3   Lending to Agriculture: 1970–1992 (in millions of dollars)

	Net Approvals	Number of Projects
Agricultural credit[a]	86.5	91
Estate development	4.3	11
Fisheries	3.0	?
Livestock	1.7	7
Crop production	34.6	31
Total	130.1	142

Source: CDB.
Note: a. Loans through financial intermediaries including agricultural production credit, farm improvement credit, and agricultural credit programs.

The pattern of lending has reflected the identified needs and
priorities of the borrowers. About two-thirds of the lending to
agriculture, both in terms of resources and the number of projects,
was for the provision of credit. Evaluation reports indicate that
these projects were satisfactory in realizing income and output
objectives but were quite poor with regard to the record of loan
repayment by farmers. The CDB plans to strengthen the loan
administration capacity of the DFCs, in order to reduce the level of
arrears.

The land settlement projects in Antigua, St. Kitts-Nevis, Barbados, St. Vincent, and Dominica were designed to reduce the uneven distribution of land ownership and to encourage more people to farm. In general, these projects have not been successful where the land was leased by the government to farmers who then did not live on the new farms. In Dominica, the government provided credit to farmers who wanted to buy the land, and these projects have been more successful.

The livestock and fisheries projects were not successful in introducing new technologies because they were too complicated for local fishermen and small farmers. In future, these projects will need to integrate production and marketing and to provide training to develop the technical and managerial skills of the beneficiaries.

In crop production, the CDB made several loans to modernize grading, packaging, and other services for export crops, and these projects have been generally more successful than those designed to stimulate domestic food production. The shifting pattern of food-crop production is making life more difficult for the small farmers who used to dominate this segment of the market. These farmers face growing competition from large sugar producers who have strong links to retail outlets and are moving into food crops as a means of agricultural diversification. Trade liberalization is flooding the market with more attractive or less costly vegetables from North America, and, under structural adjustment loans, governments are required by the World Bank, the IMF, and the IDB to end subsidized credit to small farmers.

The CDB's overall impact on the agricultural sector has been positive. The export crop development, feeder roads, and credit projects have been fairly satisfactory in realizing project objectives. Common problems have been delays in satisfying the conditions for loan effectiveness leading to higher costs, and inadequate technical, managerial, financial, and marketing skills. Sustained government support and stable management were hallmarks of the successful projects. The Belize loan portfolio, which includes projects to support the production of bananas, livestock, rice, marine fishing, and sugar, is a good illustration of the CDB's broad involvement in the agricultural sector.

In addition to loans, the Bank has provided technical assistance to pay the salaries of farm improvement officers assigned to the DFCs, and several training programs have been offered to small farmers. Other programs include institutional strengthening for the coordination of agricultural diversification in the OECS; pesticide pollution monitoring in the Windward Islands; and the services of a tropical forestry officer and strengthening of the faculty of agriculture at the University of the West Indies.

Challenges facing the sector include the reduction of production costs and development of new products and markets. The CDB's lending strategy in the 1990s is to promote sound sectoral policies, encourage more private investment, strengthen the DFCs (the principal sources of funds to the sector), and support national efforts to improve marketing, storage, transportation, and production technologies. Governments have to provide the supporting infrastructure and appropriate policy framework, but improved productivity must come from the small and medium-sized farmers who have been the focus of the CDB's support.

Priority will be given to increasing the production of export crops, and the CDB will continue to look for good fisheries projects. This sector is likely to become more important as member countries recently gained control through the Law of the Sea Convention over their exclusive economic zones. Given its importance as a source of employment and food production, agriculture and fisheries should have a larger share of future lending. However, the CDB has only two agricultural specialists on staff and expects to do only one or two agricultural projects a year. The Bank's role in direct lending to agriculture will therefore be limited and its strategy for the sector will largely be implemented through the DFCs, undertaking studies and providing technical assistance.

Industry and Tourism

Lending for industry, mining, and tourism was $268.5 million between 1970 and 1992, or about 27 percent of total lending. The CDB has financed projects in industry and tourism through direct loans to the private sector (30.1 percent), through DFCs (34.3 percent), and through public sector loans for the construction of tourist facilities and industrial estates (27.1 percent), and mining and quarrying (8.5 percent). (See Table 4.4.)

Loans to governments for the establishment of industrial estates were started in the early 1970s to provide factory shells and services to encourage manufacturing. The host governments offered generous tax incentives, allowances, and subsidized rentals to foreign firms to set up labor-intensive garment and electronics assembly operations. The program had some success in attracting firms to the region to take advantage of the preferential access offered by the United States under the Caribbean Basin

Table 4.4   Lending to Industry, Mining, and Tourism: 1970–1992

	Millions of Dollars	Percent
Indirect lending	92.2	34.3
Direct lending	176.3	65.7
Industrial estates	62.1	23.1
Food, beverages, and tobacco	37.5	14.0
Other manufacturing	24.3	9.0
Hotels and tourism	29.7	11.1
Mining	22.7	8.5
Total	268.5	100.0

Source: CDB.

Initiative (CBI) and by Canada under the Caribbean-Canada preferential tariff agreement (CARIBCAN), but several firms have recently closed their operations due to rising wage costs. The future for low-skilled, labor-intensive manufacturing in the region is not promising, and new uses will have to be found for the estates. The CDB has recommended that the management of the program should be put on a self-financing basis and separated from the activities of the DFCs.

Several of the private sector projects financed by the CDB have suffered from poor management and marketing arrangements, weak design and undercapitalization, and the repayment record has not been good. Seven private sector projects (out of fourteen in the total loan portfolio) had arrears totalling $6.2 million in October 1992, and the loans have been called. The CDB has reviewed the prospects for increased lending to the private sector and concluded that, for the time being, direct lending will be limited to $5 million a year. The commercial banks in the region are highly liquid, and medium-sized firms with good collateral have no difficulty raising funds. The CDB is exploring other avenues for assisting the private sector and will provide technical assistance for the development of entrepreneurial skills and technical and managerial ability in the region.

Development Finance Corporations (DFCs) _____

These DFCs were established by governments to assist borrowers needing longer-term or more concessional finance. Separate agencies were set up to lend to industry and agriculture; these were not adequately capitalized, had no clearly defined lending policies, and often consisted only of a manager and a secretary. Since the early 1970s, the CDB has been engaged in a program to restructure the DFCs and to put in place sound financial and operational policies. Among the steps it has taken, the Bank has provided training in project appraisal techniques; seconded banking advisers, industrial specialists, and farm improvement officers to the DFCs; recruited staff to work specifically on the DFC portfolio; and exercised careful financial supervision.

Since 1970, a quarter of the Bank's lending has been transferred through the DFCs for on-lending to the productive and social sectors—about 40 percent to agriculture and 30 percent to small industry credits and locally owned hotels. In addition, the DFCs have managed the industrial estate loans, the student loan, and mortgage financing programs. By 1992, there were twenty-seven financial intermediaries supervised by the CDB, of which fourteen were drawing down lines-of-credit.

DFC operations are staff intensive and costly to administer. Many of the subprojects are small (less than $10,000), and the CDB staff have to review dozens of proposals to find a few good projects. The viability of many of the smaller DFCs is also of concern; among the eleven currently borrowing from the CDB, five are operating profitably and six have yet to break even. The usual problems are a small asset base, weak management, and insufficient capital. The smaller DFCs have difficulty retaining good staff, and this leads to frequent slippage in project performance and loan repayment. Many are saddled with low interest rate loans and high administrative and operational costs, and they need regular government support to meet operating expenses. Many governments view the DFCs as lenders of last resort, operating where the commercial banks will not lend. As a result, the DFCs are saddled with high-risk/low-profit operations such as loans to new businesses and small farmers. Many borrowers also view the DFCs as government institutions set up to provide concessionary funds and absorb the losses.

As an alternative to DFCs, the CDB has started to channel some credit through commercial banks—through Apex institutions[1] in Jamaica and through the Central Bank in Trinidad. The Bank has also agreed on the eligibility criteria for lending to private financial institutions, but a shift to asset-based lending through commercial banks is not being considered. Commercial banks lend mostly to people who are already established, and they tend to stay in trading and construction that are less risky. DFCs can be a cost-effective mechanism for resource transfer and private sector development, and some have developed into strong institutions that are able to mobilize funds from the European Investment Bank (EIB) and bilateral donors.

The Post-Implementation and Evaluation Unit carried out an evaluation of fifty-four subprojects that benefited from five lines-of-credit provided by the CDB to the DFCs in Belize, Dominica, St. Lucia, St. Kitts/Nevis, and Grenada. The lines-of-credit were two small industry credits and three consolidated credits—farm improvement credit, agricultural production credit, agricultural and industrial credit, and mortgage finance. The objective of these credits was to channel resources to the poorest farmers and to encourage small-scale industrial activities. Nineteen of the subprojects were in agriculture and twenty-two in manufacturing.

The evaluation reports indicate that the objectives of the credits were achieved in terms of transferring resources to the lowest income groups, increasing employment and output, and providing technical assistance to strengthen the DFCs. The principal problems encountered were weaknesses in loan administration and the need for more supervision. Some subborrowers did not observe loan conditions with regard to buying insurance and keeping regular accounts; others were delinquent in making loan repayments even when their projects were successful. The evaluations suggested that the staff of the DFCs need continuous training on project analysis and loan administration, and that the CDB needs to spend more time and resources on the supervision of DFCs and the subborrowers.

The CDB intends to put increased emphasis on the financial viability of the DFCs and will ask governments to increase their equity contributions. The Bank will no longer assign full-time staff to the DFCs but will provide short-term consultants and training in project analysis. Five of the specialists assigned to the DFCs were hired by the CDB, and the six advisers were hired by the DFCs. Increased attention will be given to the lending policies, financial practices, and management of the DFCs, and the training in project appraisal will be complemented by training in banking and loan administration. The objective is to encourage the DFCs to become self-financing, to show a rate of return on assets, reduce the foreign exchange risk, and improve on their loan collections. Improvements will also be made in the CDB's management of the DFC portfolio through the expanded use of consolidated lines-of-credit, and more autonomy will be given to the staff of the DFCs for project selection. Efforts are under way to computerize DFC operations to improve monitoring and to standardize appraisals, and CDB staff will spend more time on supervision.

The DFCs have been crucial to the functioning of the CDB. Without them, the Bank would not have been able to carry out its mandate in the LDCs or to reach small farmers and entrepreneurs. Lending through the DFCs helped to strengthen the financial infrastructure in the region; it played an important role in promoting grassroots development and provided a mechanism for delivering emergency rehabilitation aid after the hurricanes. However, in view of the high cost of operating more than twenty-five DFCs in the region, consideration should be given to the suggestion made by President William Demas in his 1977 annual meeting speech—that there should have been only one DFC for the OECS countries, with branches on each island.[2] Advances in information processing technology should be used by the CDB to improve the way it manages its DFC portfolio and by the governments of the OECS countries to facilitate the consolidation of their small DFCs into one.

Regional Projects

The CDB is required by its Charter to promote economic cooperation and integration among its members, and it has financed regional projects in agriculture, industry, and transport. The first regional loan was made in 1974 to the publicly owned West Indian Shipping Corporation (WISCO) for the purchase of a container vessel for traffic between the MDCs. Further loans were made in 1980 and 1984 to buy two vessels for the Eastern Caribbean route. The first loan to LIAT, the regional airline Leeward Islands Air Transport, was made in 1975 and further loans were made in 1979 and in 1984. Poor management, low traffic volumes, and under capitalization were common problems, and neither of these projects has been successful. WISCO is in receivership, and the CDB is providing technical assistance on the privatization of LIAT.

In 1975, two regional grain projects were approved. The Guyana project—jointly owned by the governments of Guyana, St. Kitts-Nevis, and Trinidad and Tobago—was designed to produce and process soybeans, corn, and black-eyed peas in Guyana. A similar project owned by Belize and Jamaica was located in Belize. Both projects experienced financial and implementation problems due to the lack of economies of scale, inadequate guarantees from governments, poorly trained staff, and undercapitalization.

Feasibility studies on regional fisheries and livestock projects were carried out, and, to avoid some of the problems of the grain projects, the CDB provided financing for national projects producing for the regional market. However, these projects were also unsuccessful. They suffered from management, design, and cost escalation problems; inadequate marketing arrangements; and the lack of local technical expertise. In the 1980s, no new regional projects were approved, but the CDB continued to provide technical assistance grants to carry out regional studies and training programs such as the Agricultural Diversification and Input Supply Study for the OECS, the Power Loss Reduction Study, and the regional water management and training program. In 1992, the CDB cofinanced a project with the IDB to strengthen the University of the West Indies and support a distance learning project in the region.

Social Sectors

The CDB's involvement in the social sectors has been mainly through the provision of mortgage financing for low- and middle-income housing, the provision of student loans, and the Basic Needs Trust Fund (BNTF) Program. The student loan program was started in 1972 to finance postprimary and postsecondary education in the LDCs and to support the growth of regional training institutions. The program is administered by the DFCs following guidelines established by the CDB. The subloans to students carry interest rates of 8 percent, with a grace period covering the period of study and maturities of ten years.

During 1972–1991, the CDB approved forty-nine student loans to twelve LDCs amounting to $18.2 million, 45 percent of which was approved over the past four years. The largest share went to St. Kitts-Nevis (23 percent), followed by Dominica (19 percent), and St. Lucia (15 percent). The program has enabled 2,500 students to make counterpart contributions to training programs financed through scholarships or family finances. On average, the CDB provided 35 percent of the cost of the training programs.

An evaluation of the student loan program in 1988 showed that it had made a significant contribution to human resource development in the region, to the benefit of both the students and their employers. Almost half of the students were women, and 60 percent were under the age of twenty-five. Problems encountered included the high rate of emigration of the borrowers (39 percent) and the high rate of arrears (44 percent); the two were often related. In recent years, an increasing number of students have asked for extraregional training in degree courses rather than vocational training within the region. These students often do not return, and those who do come back have experienced problems finding jobs that pay enough to service the loans.

The student loan program is highly regarded because it enables qualified students from less-well-off families to pursue higher education. The demand for loans currently exceeds supply by 50 percent, but before additional resources are put into the program, the guidelines for approved courses should be reviewed to give preference to the upgrading of skills within the region, to reduce operating costs, and increase loan repayments. Special efforts should be made to encourage students to stay in the region and to provide soft loans to qualified students from poor families who are excluded from the program because they cannot provide counterpart funds.

The Basic Needs Trust Fund (BNTF) program was started in 1984 with a contribution of $12.7 million from USAID and $3.5 million from the CDB; it received an additional contribution of $10 million in 1988. Its objective was to alleviate the hardships of the most vulnerable groups in the OECS countries and to expand and conserve, through the use of labor-intensive techniques, the stock of social and economic capital. The BNTF finances projects in health, education, water supply, drainage, rural roads, and retail trading facilities such as farm outlets, fishermen's wharves, and so on. The projects are labor-intensive and fast-disbursing, and governments are always willing to provide the needed counterpart funds. BNTF projects do not exceed $500,000 in total cost, and most are much smaller. By 1992, 252 projects had been approved, and, of these, 242 have been implemented and 239 have been completed. This is a significant accomplishment, and it highlights the program's overall success.

The BNTF program targets an important socioeconomic issue—high rates of unemployment. It has a high profile in the beneficiary countries and is much appreciated. An evaluation by independent consultants for USAID found the program to be well conceived and worthwhile: "greatly exceeding the targets for employment generation and project execution," as one USAID official stated in an interview. However, an important weakness is the lack of arrangements to ensure proper maintenance and replacement. Experience in other developing countries indicates that local communities must become more involved in the design and maintenance of these projects if they are to be sustainable. The projects must include a training component to teach the community how to carry out routine repairs and maintenance, and the community should be assisted in establishing a fund to raise money for repairs and replacement. Unless the communities accept ownership of the projects, they become a burden on the budget.

Evaluation and supervision reports indicate that the best response to the program has been in St. Vincent; the ministry of public works builds schools, health centers, and rural roads and is concerned that the projects are well carried out. In Dominica and Grenada, the ministry of finance is the official executing agency, but other agencies carry out the projects; this increases the need for interagency coordination. The projects in St. Lucia have encountered problems of cost escalation and delays due to a construction boom on the island.

BNTF projects would not qualify for World Bank or IDB funding because they are too small and their financial rates of return would probably not justify a loan. The CDB does not calculate rates of return on these projects but takes note of the project benefits and the employment generation, health, and education aspects. The second phase of the BNTF program funded by USAID came to an end in September 1992, and USAID agreed to a further grant of $2 million to extend the program for another two years. The CDB has initiated a third phase for selected OECS/Group III countries (Belize and Guyana with an allocation of $15 million from the special development fund); it is looking for additional contributors. In the absence of matching funds from external sources, the CDB will ask beneficiary countries to cofinance projects in domestic currencies in the ratio of one-third to two-thirds from the SDF.

Notes

1. Second-story institutions that on-lend through several approved financial institutions including commercial banks.
2. "Experience over the past six years indicates that it might have been better for the CDB to have aimed at the establishment of a single DFC for all seven Leeward and Windward Islands with branches in each island. For not only would such an institution have economized on scarce personnel at the top and middle levels but it might have been able to undertake—on a subregional basis—many of the industrial promotion tasks with which some individual DFCs have been struggling at the national level." Speech at the annual meeting of the Board of Governors, April 1977.

5

COUNTRY STUDIES

The OECS Countries

When the CDB was established, it was given a mandate to pay special attention to the needs of the smaller countries that were perceived as lagging behind in their development. Its impact on the region can best be gauged by a review of loans to the OECS countries that have received 55 percent of total lending and 85 percent of the technical assistance grants since 1970.[1] These newly independent countries had been heavily reliant on budget support from the United Kingdom, and they lacked the administrative and technical capacity to prepare and implement projects. As a result, considerable effort and resources were spent by the CDB in the early years on preparing projects, restructuring the DFCs, training, and institution-building. The agricultural and industrial credit programs were initiated in the OECS countries and Belize, as were schemes for industrial estates, feeder roads, urban working class housing, and student loans. In response to the global crisis in the 1970s, the CDB helped to establish the Fund for Emergency Programmes and Common Services to provide balance-of-payments support to OECS countries. (See Table 5.1.)

GDP growth in the OECS countries was relatively flat during the 1970s; however, major investments in infrastructure took place that laid the foundation for later rapid growth, and most of these investments were financed by the CDB on soft terms. The projects included the expansion of ports, intraregional transport, power generation and transmission, and road rehabilitation. During the 1980s, the OECS countries achieved GDP growth rates of 5 percent per annum, and, by the end of the decade, per capita incomes ranged from about $5,000 in Antigua and Barbuda to $1,620 for St. Vincent and the Grenadines.

Table 5.1   Distribution of Loans and Grants by Country and Fund: 1970–1992
(in millions of dollars)

Country	Ordinary Capital Resources	Special Fund Resources	Total	Percent
Anguilla	3.5	9.2	12.7	1.2
Antigua and Barbuda	4.0	13.0	17.0	1.6
Bahamas	66.2	3.7	69.9	6.4
Barbados	46.0	22.2	68.2	6.2
Belize	11.7	63.7	75.4	6.9
British Virgin Islands	12.4	15.8	28.2	2.6
Cayman Islands	29.8	8.5	38.3	3.5
Dominica	10.7	72.6	83.3	7.6
Grenada	7.1	50.8	57.9	5.3
Guyana	22.2	74.5	96.7	8.8
Jamaica	105.1	76.7	181.8	16.5
Montserrat	3.7	9.7	13.4	1.2
St. Kitts-Nevis	13.7	46.0	59.7	5.4
St. Lucia	23.4	67.3	90.7	8.2
St. Vincent and the Grenadines	9.0	62.7	71.7	6.5
Trinidad and Tobago	49.5	3.7	53.2	4.8
Turks and Caicos	2.5	6.1	8.6	0.8
Regional	7.4	66.4	73.8	6.7
Total	427.9	672.6	1,100.5	
Percent	38.9	61.1		100.0

Source: CDB.

Tourism led in growth, and it helped to stimulate activity in other sectors; agriculture came next, with light manufacturing and financial, construction, and other services playing a significant role in some countries. Agriculture boomed in the Windward Islands (Dominica, Grenada, St. Lucia, and St. Vincent and the Grenadines) in the 1980s with the expansion of banana exports but declined in the Leeward islands (St. Kitts-Nevis, Antigua and Barbuda, and Montserrat) with the steady decline of the sugar industry. Manufacturing accounts for only about 7 percent of GDP (except in St. Lucia where it accounts for 13.5 percent) and consists largely of light manufactures for export, the processing of agricultural commodities, and consumer goods assembly. The CDB provided assistance in developing the infrastructure to facilitate the growth of tourism, in supporting the expansion of banana exports and in the establishment of industrial estates.

Macroeconomic policy in the OECS is guided by the Antigua-based Economic Affairs Secretariat of the OECS and the Eastern Caribbean Central Bank (ECCB), with its headquarters in St. Kitts-

Nevis. Members of the OECS share a common currency managed by the ECCB, and the exchange rate, which is pegged to the U.S. dollar, can only be altered by unanimous agreement. Tight monetary policies and prudent fiscal management have helped the OECS countries to maintain a stable exchange rate and low inflation.

The CDB has played an important role in improving public sector finances in the subregion. All OECS countries had difficulty balancing their budgets in the 1970s and early 1980s, but by 1990 all except Grenada and Antigua and Barbuda were in surplus. The major sources of government revenue are customs duties, and other indirect taxes, and tourist taxes; savings, therefore, had to come from restraining the growth of public expenditure. The CDB assisted in the preparation of public sector investment programs (PSIPs) and required public utilities to charge tariffs to cover their costs. The recent trend in the OECS countries has been for national savings to finance an increasing share of their gross investment; this is not the case in the larger Caribbean countries.

Capital investment is financed mainly by foreign private flows, grants, and soft loans. The debt and debt service ratios of the OECS are low, except for Grenada and Antigua and Barbuda. Despite their sound economic performance and high levels of per capita income, the financing of future investment is a problem for the OECS countries; they are no longer eligible for IDA funds but are not creditworthy for commercial loans due to the extreme volatility of their export earnings and low tax-base.

The external environment for trade and aid may not be as favorable in the 1990s, and greater attention will have to be given to increasing the efficiency of investment and raising national savings. High wages will hamper the growth of manufacturing output, and agricultural diversification is being stressed to counter the possible loss of preferential markets for bananas. The main activity will continue to be tourism. The number of tourists has increased at 7 percent per annum over the past five years The OECS countries have increased their share of Caribbean and worldwide traffic, but the volume is still very low (5–6 percent of Caribbean traffic and 0.1 percent of world traffic), which leaves room for further growth. However, the rapid development of tourism is likely to exacerbate existing environmental problems— the erosion of beaches, destruction of coral reefs, and water pollution. The small size of the OECS countries increases their vulnerability, and they do not have the technical personnel or the financial resources needed for environmental protection.

Human resource development is another urgent priority in the OECS countries. High population growth rates and a young, mostly unskilled labor force have contributed to high rates of unemployment (15–35 percent) on some islands. The unemployment problem is compounded by the low overall quality of education. Failure rates are 40–50 percent in primary and secondary schools; teachers are mostly untrained, and the equipment and buildings are inadequate. More resources have to be directed to expanding enrollment in secondary, technical, and vocational education and in raising the number of qualified university applicants. The CDB has provided assistance to education in the OECS, but, given the magnitude of the problem and the high per capita costs of providing education, more assistance will be needed in the future.

Generally, the LDCs (including the dependencies) have performed better than the MDCs over the past decade despite a deterioration in their terms of trade, the fluctuations in world output, and inclement weather. The CDB cannot be given the credit for their success since the OECS countries were the beneficiaries of substantial inflows of concessionary finance, a dynamic tourist industry, and preferential access to markets for their principal exports. However, the CDB contributed in no small measure in helping these countries take advantage of the opportunities available to them.

St. Lucia
(Population 151,000; 1990 Average Per Capita Income $2,414)

St. Lucia's real GDP expanded at 5 percent per annum over the past decade, with steady growth in tourism, manufacturing, and agricultural output. GDP growth declined in 1991 to about 3 percent due to a prolonged drought that resulted in a 25 percent drop in banana sales. Manufacturing output was also constrained by the lack of trade financing, skilled labor, and marketing know-how. These declines were partially offset by a 27 percent increase in the number of visitors. The recurrent budget showed a surplus of EC $65 million, and external debt increased from $55 million to $70 million due to increased public sector borrowing. St. Lucia's medium-term prospects for continued growth are good because of its relatively diversified economy and strong fiscal performance.

Between 1970 and 1991, St. Lucia received loans from the CDB totalling $82.8 million; agriculture received $12 million, manufacturing $21.4 million, tourism $5 million, water $14.8 million, transportation $18.6 million, housing $4.2 million, and education $6.8

million. A 1983 small farmers diversification loan of $1.1 million to provide marketing facilities resulted in a near doubling of the volume of produce marketed in three years. Recent CDB projects include the fourth airport project ($8 million); the eighth industrial estate loan ($5.2 million); the fifth student loan ($1 million), and a technical assistance grant of $415,600 to strengthen the Department of Statistics.

About 40 percent of the lending was channelled through the St. Lucia Development Bank, which received a third line-of-credit from the CDB for $4 million in 1991. The bank operates independently of government, and staff turnover is low; a farm improvement officer whose salary was paid by the CDB for the past ten years has recently been hired by the bank. Commercial banks are not competitors, but they have an advantage in that they are security-based lending institutions, and they make decisions more quickly. The Bank is financially sound, but it needs additional equity to ensure future growth. Arrears account for only 3 percent of the loan portfolio, and the biggest problem is the loss from foreign currency fluctuations. External sources of funding are the CDB, the European Investment Bank (EIB), and France.

The CDB has made loans to the St. Lucia Electricity Corporation (LUCELEC), an electricity corporation that operates profitably and plans to make its shares available to the public. The government holds 48 percent of the shares, and the Commonwealth Development Corporation (CDC) holds 52 percent. Since 1982, the company has negotiated loans directly with the CDB and has received support from the Bank on setting tariffs and collecting overdue bills from other government agencies. A major expansion of the service is under way to provide electricity to the rural areas and to replace old equipment, and in 1990 a new power station was commissioned with funds from the EIB and CDC for a total cost of E.C. $100 million.

The CDB has made loans for road rehabilitation and financed feeder roads to facilitate the delivery of bananas. The port authority, which has benefited from CDB funding and the provision of technical assistance and training, is well run and has accumulated reserves since 1982. In an interview, one port official considered the CDB "a valuable regional institution, staffed with competent people who are easily accessible." They said that it would not have been possible to obtain information on the cost of building the airport in Belize from any other institution but the CDB, and that this information had been useful to the government in considering its own airport expansion.

Officials interviewed suggested that the CDB should play a greater role in promoting financial cooperation among the OECS countries; provide more training in the preparation of PSIPs and on the project cycle; and act as a catalyst for capital market development. The CDB should also continue to provide advice on the design of medium-term adjustment programs in conjunction with other regional institutions, as in the case of Grenada; should look at more regional projects; and should help develop a strategy for the region in agro-industry and in tourism. The only criticism concerned the CDB's lengthy loan processing procedures. It was recognized that the Bank could not finance very large or complex projects such as the Roseau Dam, which has a total cost of E.C. $100 million and is being financed by the World Bank and the Canadian International Development Agency (CIDA). Nevertheless, a St. Lucia official felt that the CDB's projects department needed strengthening because "it is stretched thin and its delivery capacity is slow." The CDB had done well in the traditional areas of transport, public utilities, communications, and agriculture and needed to develop new areas of expertise such as the environment, small business development, housing, and finance.

St. Vincent and the Grenadines
(Population 118,000; 1990 Average Per Capita Income $1,620)

St. Vincent and the Grenadines has registered real GDP growth of over 6 percent per annum in the past decade. Agriculture accounts for 26 percent of GDP, construction 18 percent, tourism 12 percent, and manufacturing 8 percent. St. Vincent is the only OECS country beside Dominica with a large agricultural sector, and most of the growth of output was due to the 60 percent expansion of banana acreage and the increase in yields resulting from greater applications of pesticides and fertilizers.

GDP growth has slowed since 1990 due to a sharp drop in manufacturing output. The doubling of the minimum wage paid to women in 1989 may have been a factor in the closing of the largest enterprise, a sporting goods firm producing for export. The fall in manufacturing output was partially offset by increases in tourism and construction. Improved marketing resulted in a 23 percent increase in tourists, with cruise-ship passengers increasing by 58 percent. Construction activity was boosted by high levels of public sector investment and homebuilding. The improvement in the management of public finances was reflected in the shift in public sector savings from a small deficit in 1983 to a surplus of 3 percent of GDP in 1992. Total debt outstanding in 1990 was $54 million or 29 percent of GDP, and the debt service ratio was 3 percent.

The expansion of cultivated acreage into the watershed areas is causing concern, and the government is giving priority to raising agricultural productivity. The island has enormous potential for tourism, but substantial investments are needed to expand and upgrade the airport and tourist facilities. High priority is also being given to education and training to address the problem of unemployment, which is officially estimated at 20–25 percent of the labor force, and the low skill-mix.

Between 1970 and 1991, St. Vincent received loans from the CDB totalling $63.2 million—agriculture received $15.9 million, manufacturing $19 million, mining $4.4 million, power $6.6 million, water $2.6 million, transportation $7.9 million, housing $2.6 million, and education $3.9 million. Recent loans include a second line of credit to the development bank ($2.5 million); a second water supply project ($1.16 million); a project to convert a large government estate (Orange Hill) into a settlement of 600 farming families; and $4.3 million loan for quarry development to halt the use of beach sand in construction.

The CDB made four loans for the construction of feeder roads that have increased the area under cultivation and facilitated the movement of bananas, but more attention needs to be given in the future to road maintenance and improvement. Loans to the power sector were channelled through the St. Vincent Electricity Corporation (VINLEC), a corporation that is wholly owned by the government and that the government is seeking to privatize. Tariffs cover costs, and the company is efficiently managed. The government has been able to borrow from the EIB at 5 percent and on-lend the funds to the corporation at 7.5 percent at a time when interest rates on CDB loans averaged 9–10 percent.

The port authority is also a statutory corporation that is profitably run and has accumulated a surplus. The agency is considering very large investments and is looking at the CDB and other sources to finance its expansion plans. A CDB loan that was not successful was the E.C. $0.75 million provided for a deep-water pier expansion (Berthing Dolphin). The extension gave 150 feet of extra berthing space for cruise-ships, but the pier was not used because passengers had to pass through the cargo handling area. A plan to build a walkway to avoid the cargo area was never implemented.

The Development Bank of St. Vincent (DEVCO) borrows from

the CDB and the EIB for on-lending and receives revenue for industrial estate management and from loans. The bank has had problems with high-level staff retainment and with chronic arrears on its small farming and industrial loans. Drought, poor marketing, and poor management are the most frequently cited reasons for late payments. DEVCO has also suffered losses from currency fluctuations and is looking for additional equity from the government and a new line-of-credit from the CDB.

St. Vincent and the Grenadines "values its relationship with the CDB which provides in excess of 50 percent of its external financing needs and valuable technical assistance in vital areas of the economy," according to a St. Vincent official in an interview. The PSIP is prepared every year with the help of the CDB and the World Bank at the same time as the budget, and it identifies the projects to be financed. The training and technical assistance offered by the CDB and the Caribbean Technological Consultancy Services have been beneficial to small businesses, and the Basic Needs Trust Fund Program has provided social and infrastructure facilities that have improved the quality of life for both the rural and urban poor. A St. Vincent official stated in an interview that the only criticism of the CDB relates to the fact that it "operates like the World Bank in dumping currencies which it holds in excess and demanding repayment in the currency disbursed or the U.S. $."

St. Kitts-Nevis
(Population 43,000; 1990 Average Per Capita Income $3,559)

During the 1980s, aided by the strong growth of tourism and construction, real GDP in St. Kitts-Nevis averaged 4–5 percent per annum. In 1989, Hurricane Hugo caused severe damage; and in 1990 and 1991, GDP growth slowed down to around 3 percent. St. Kitts-Nevis has a low level of external debt, low inflation, and the budget shows a current account surplus. The outlook for growth is good, but the country needs to resolve land tenure issues, strengthen its infrastructure, and mobilize more domestic resources for development.

Between 1970 and 1991, St. Kitts-Nevis received loans from the CDB totalling $41 million—agriculture received $3.8 million, manufacturing $7.4 million, power $5.3 million, transport $10.7 million, housing $6.5 million, and education $5.6 million. About two-thirds of the loans were for infrastructure projects (feeder roads, construction, sea defense, ports, and electricity expansion), and most of the projects appear to have met their performance targets. The port authority is a profitably run statutory body, and a recent loan for the construction of the ferry pier downtown will provide more berthing space for cruise-ships. A loan of E.C. $21.79 million to the power sector will finance the expansion and upgrading of services and the establishment of an electricity corporation. Two current public works projects are the resurfacing of sixteen miles of the island's ring road and the rehabilitation of a building adjacent to government headquarters.

In the directly productive sectors, the CDB has provided assistance for the modernization of the sugar industry and the development of nontraditional crops; manufacturing has been assisted through four loans for industrial estates. Two loans totalling $1.5 million, financed the development of a tourism center, and construction has been helped by loans for housing, hurricane rehabilitation, and hotel construction.

The CDB has made several loans to the Development Bank of St. Kitts, which was established in 1981 when it took over the assets and liabilities of the DFC that existed between 1968 and 1980. Staff turnover in the bank is low, and the quality of the loan portfolio is fairly good. The bank operates profitably but needs an injection of equity capital of about U.S. $2 million over the next three years to ensure further growth. In addition to funding, the CDB provides technical advice through the Caribbean Technological Consultancy Services network, and an advisor who also trains staff has been attached to the bank and paid for by the CDB. The bank manages four industrial estates, but these are administratively costly; the CDB has suggested that this function be taken over by another agency. The development bank also manages secondary mortgage financing and student loans.

Assistance provided to the social sectors has included mortgage financing and the recent loan of $2 million for shelter development to benefit low-income families, the technical/vocational education project that the CDB cofinanced with the World Bank, and student loans. The Basic Needs Trust Fund finances small projects such as minor repairs to village roads and provision of a day-care center.

Interviews with various government officials and project officers indicated high regard for the CDB's contribution to the country and the region. There were complaints that the procedures for making loans, tendering, and procurement are too cumbersome and that the CDB often acts more like a commercial bank than a development bank, but the general consensus was that the CDB was valuable because of its proximity and familiarity with the region. The staff of the CDB were held in high regard, and working relationships were less impersonal than those with the other international financial institutions (IFIs) or donor agencies; it was less costly doing business with the CDB because the loan negotiations take place in the country or in Barbados.

Grenada
(Population 100,000; 1990 Average Per Capita Income $2,000)

From 1984 to 1990, real GDP grew at over 6 percent per annum, fuelled by strong growth in tourism, construction, and manufacturing; these contributed 15 percent, 11 percent, and 6 percent respectively to GDP. The growth of tourism was helped by the construction of the new airport and several new hotels, and manufacturing was supported by tax concessions and increased access to the U.S. market through the Caribbean Basin Initiative. Agriculture accounts for 15 percent of total output, and the principal crops are nutmeg, mace, bananas, and cocoa.

Inflation has averaged under 3 percent per annum, and the government has made major efforts to control spending and raise revenues. Public sector savings increased from a deficit in the early 1980s to a surplus of 7 percent of GDP in 1988. Since then, the budget has been under pressure due to the decline in net capital inflows and increased spending. Wages in the private sector increased by 33 percent between 1983 and 1988 because of the acute shortage of labor, and, in 1989, the government granted an across-the-board wage increase of 22 percent to public sector workers to maintain parity with the private sector. Despite measures to raise revenues, the deficit widened in 1990 to E.C. $18.6 million and was financed primarily through an accumulation of arrears on external debt. At the end of 1990, Grenada's total debt stood at $80 million or 48 percent of GDP. Debt service equalled 10 percent of exports and 19 percent of government revenues, and arrears amounted to $20.4 million.

GDP growth slowed down in 1991 to 3 percent per annum. Tourism growth was strong, but there was a sharp decline in agriculture due to the rise in nonagricultural wages and uncertain export markets. Construction activity was dampened by the sharp decline in public sector investment. These declines were partly offset by the doubling in the number of tourists from 1989 to 1991 and increases in manufacturing output. The weak fiscal performance continued in 1991 and led to a further buildup in arrears on debt service. During 1991, the government received assistance from four regional institutions (CDB, ECCB, OECS Secretariat, and UWI) in the preparation of a medium-term adjustment program. The director of the CDB's Economic Department led the team that helped Grenada to draft a program emphasizing the need for tight fiscal management, broadening of the revenue base, and debt restructuring.

Prospects for growth depend on the performance of agriculture and the tourist sector. Grenada has considerable potential for tourism, but, with a hotel occupancy rate of under 50 percent, further investment in capacity is not needed. Attention must be given to improved marketing, upgrading the quality of services, and environmental protection. Grand Anse, the major beach, and its offshore reef are threatened by sewage from the capital and leakages from individually installed septic tanks. Consideration should be given to limiting development on Grand Anse until the problems of pollution and beach erosion have been addressed.

Between 1970 and 1991, Grenada received loans from the CDB totalling $56 million; agriculture received $16.6 million, manufacturing $6.5 million, tourism $4.0 million, water $2.3 million, transport $11.6 million, housing $3.9 million, and education $3.7 million. Grenada has also received technical assistance and training from the CDB and over $15 million to fund basic needs projects. Recent CDB loans include a $3.4 million multipurpose project loan for the Grenadines; a $4 million loan for hotel development; a $5.16 million loan to build 19.2 km of feeder roads serving 900 farming families; a second line-of-credit ($5 million) to the development bank; and a $6 million loan for road rehabilitation. The loans for the construction of feeder roads have supported agricultural development, but the three roads that were completed by 1989 are being inadequately maintained due to lack of funds.

The development bank has shown a small profit despite a chronic state of arrears, particularly on its loans for agricultural and hotel development. The bank is trying to eliminate the arrears and is asking the government for an infusion of equity in order to borrow E.C. $50 million from the CDB over the next five years. Bank officials feel that the training provided by the CDB in project preparation needs to be given more frequently and that increased supervision by the CDB would be beneficial. A farm improvement officer whose salary has been paid by the CDB has been attached to the bank for the past sixteen years.

The port authority became a statutory body in 1982 and is a financially sound institution that has accumulated a surplus.

There have been no recent CDB loans, but the agency hopes to borrow from the CDB in the future. The Grenada Electricity Corporation (GRENLEC) is a private electricity company that supplies 94 percent of the island with electricity. The tariffs charged cover costs and provide a rate of return of 4–8 percent, but this is not enough to cover future investments or contributions to the employees' pension fund. The officials interviewed felt that the CDB had a better understanding of the problems of the region than the larger MDBs. They cited the Power Loss Reduction Study conducted by the CDB for the region that was considered better than the studies done by foreign consultants. Most of the study's recommendations have been implemented, and the government is looking for a buyer for GRENLEC.

Barbados (Population 257,400; 1990 Average Per Capita Income $6,000)

Barbados experienced steady GDP growth at 4.7 percent per annum during the 1970s, but economic growth was slow and uneven during the 1980s. Output fell in 1981–1982, stabilized in 1983, and averaged 3.2 percent per annum between 1984 and 1989. The share of agriculture, manufacturing, and mining fell from 18 percent to 14 percent over 1985–1990, and services constitute over two-thirds of GDP. The government is the largest employer, accounting for 23.1 percent of the workforce in 1990, followed by manufacturing (10.5 percent), construction (8 percent), and tourism (8.7 percent). Throughout the decade, unemployment was high, averaging 15–16 percent. In 1990, GDP fell by 3.3 percent, the fiscal deficit rose to 8.8 percent of GDP, and unemployment increased to 17.9 percent. At the end of 1990, total external debt stood at $542 million, or 31 percent of GDP, and the debt service ratio was 25 percent.

Sugar is no longer the dominant sector but is still important to the economy, accounting for 22 percent of export earnings and 5 percent of employment. The industry faces severe problems due to weak demand and production costs that are 30 percent above the world average. Barbados has been unable to produce enough sugar to meet preferential quota sales on the EU and U.S. markets; as a result, these quotas have been declining. Since 1982, the government has supported Barbados Sugar Industries Limited (BSIL), the privately owned consortium that processes all the sugar. In 1991, BSIL experienced serious financial difficulties and almost had to cease operations because it could not service its debt of U.S. $87.5 million. The book value of its assets was only $12–$15 million. A rescue package has been arranged by Booker Tate of London; the company will assume management and inject new capital, provided the government writes off over one-third of the debt.

Tourism is the major sector accounting for 11 percent of GDP and about 45 percent of export earnings, but the industry has recently suffered a number of setbacks. Over the decade, Barbados lost a quarter of its share of the Caribbean traffic but managed to increase its share of tourist expenditure because it has more year-round visitors with longer stayovers than the other islands. Since 1989, tourist arrivals have fallen by 15 percent, and the hotel occupancy rate has dropped below 50 percent. The industry has been severely hurt by the closure of three major airlines that had frequent flights from North America to Bridgetown.

A decline in manufacturing is due to high labor costs and poor trading conditions. A promising development is the shift to data processing for several major airlines and insurance companies; this earned $50 million in 1991 and employed 1,600 persons.

Throughout the 1980s, the budget registered deficits that were financed by commercial borrowing. However, fiscal imbalance and pressure on the trade account eroded the country's ability to borrow. The drying up of commercial bank loans and sizeable capital outflows resulted in increased reliance on domestic financing and a drawing down of reserves. Total external debt in 1991 was $614 million or 31 percent of GDP; debt service payments were 20 percent of export earnings and 22 percent of government revenues.

Output fell by 4.5 percent in 1991, unemployment soared to 20 percent, and prices rose by 6.3 percent. With economic activity slowing, foreign reserves falling, and a heavy debt burden, the government began discussions with the IMF for a standby program. In the austerity budget of September 1991, the government announced sharp spending cuts, increased taxes and user fees, layoffs, reduced transfers to public enterprises, deferment of capital works, and the sale of assets. These corrective measures reduced the deficit from 7.5 percent of GDP in 1991 to 1 percent in 1992 and contributed to a rebuilding of gross reserves.

Economic recovery is likely to be slow. The prospects for sugar are bleak and manufacturing output is constrained by high costs. The outlook for the growth of tourism is uncertain as well. Greater attention is being given to marketing and raising the quality of tourism services, but, in addition to higher airfares, the average cost of a vacation in Barbados is higher than in Antigua, Jamaica, or the Bahamas. A sustained recovery will require major policy changes, improvements in labor productivity, and a restoration of competitiveness. On the plus side, Barbados has a highly developed social and economic infrastructure, a well-educated workforce, and a stable political environment that should facilitate the implementation of the required policy changes.

Barbados has not been a major borrower from the CDB. Between 1970 and 1991, loan approvals totalled $67.1 million or 7.2 percent of total bank lending; most of the loans came from the CDB's ordinary capital resources. Loans totalling $15 million from the USAID-financed Caribbean Development Facility (CDF) and Basic Human Needs (BHN) programs provided the bulk of the concessional financing. Almost all the loans have been to the public sector: about 37 percent went to the agriculture and manufacturing sectors and 63 percent to transport, communications, and education. The CDB made three loans for agricultural credit and land settlement; four loans for the establishment of industrial estates; two loans for airport rehabilitation; and three loans for road construction.

The performance of the loan portfolio has been mixed. Postevaluation reports suggest that only the infrastructure projects were relatively problem-free, tending to confirm the CDB's success in this sector. The other projects, in varying degrees, experienced delays and cost overruns at the implementation stage and management, marketing, and financial problems at the operational stage. The Spring Hall Land Lease Project and the Airport Rehabilitation Project provide a sharp contrast. The Spring Hall Land Lease Project, approved in 1979, was for the settlement of twenty-two tenants on more than 400 acres of land. The loan of $928,000 was to be used to develop farms, provide irrigation facilities, establish an equipment pool and management services, and provide credit. The project was adversely affected by design problems and by structural changes in the sector that resulted in delays in implementation and cost overruns exceeding $1 million. Disbursement was slow: after nine years, only 25 percent of the project area had been cultivated and 76 percent of the farms occupied. On the other hand, the Airport Rehabilitation Project was fully implemented on schedule at a cost of roughly $2 million below the appraisal estimate. Approved in 1985, $7 million was provided for the reconstruction of one section of the runway, the strengthening and resurfacing of other sections, drainage works, landscaping, and the installation of aviation lighting.

Apart from loans and technical assistance, Barbados derives

other benefits from the CDB. In the late 1960s, the government made strenuous efforts to get the CDB located in Barbados, which provided the land and met the cost of the original office building. This fitted into the strategy to make Bridgetown the "Geneva of the Caribbean." The regional offices of the UNDP, Pan-American Health Organisation (PAHO), and Food and Agriculture Organization (FAO) were later located in Barbados and the regional marketing arms of Texaco and Shell relocated from Trinidad. This cluster of international institutions and corporations helps to promote Barbados as a stable international financial center and is an important source of foreign exchange earnings.

The location of the CDB's headquarters in Barbados has other benefits for the island. The administrative expenses of the CDB in 1991 were approximately $8.5 million, including expenditure on salaries, supplies, printing, and telecommunications. The central bank derives benefits from the provision of depository services and from the not insignificant "float" on foreign exchange deposits awaiting disbursement to borrowers. Another important, though nonquantifiable benefit, is the presence of the CDB's high quality professional staff, who have shown over the past twenty-two years that regional institutions can achieve high international standards of performance.

The recent deterioration in the economic environment has brought about a closer relationship between the CDB and Barbados. The government's approach to the IMF in 1991 initiated an intensive policy dialogue with the multilateral lending institutions, including the CDB. In response, the CDB has accelerated lending to Barbados and has recently made a large loan for the revitalization of the sugar industry. The public sector investment program for the fiscal years 1992/93 to 1996/97 envisages a bigger role for the CDB, with the contribution as high as 10 percent of projected capital expenditure or 15 percent of the required external resources. However, over the medium term, project lending may be constrained by the inability of the public sector to provide counterpart financing and meet debt service payments.

A more important role for the CDB in the future will be to help redirect the focus of government economic policies. For the past four decades, the government has played a major role in the country's economic progress. The implementation of sound macroeconomic policies, a supportive role for the private sector, and good governance were complemented by large expenditures on the installation of a modern infrastructure and the provision of educational, health, and other social services. However, over the past decade it became increasingly evident that a major shift was needed in the role of the government. In 1990, government expenditure was 40 percent of GDP, but there is now very little need for new investment in infrastructure or a significant expansion in social services. The improvements needed are qualitative not quantitative—to increase the efficiency of resource use and investments through improved management and better policies. A reduced role for the government entails privatization of state enterprises, management reform, the restoration of the independence and high level of competence of the civil service, and support for an increased role for the private sector. The CDB can help to foster private sector development, but it has an even more important advisory role to play in helping Barbados to make the structural changes and policy shifts required for economic recovery.

Guyana (Population 760,000; 1990 Average Per Capita Income $370)

The economic deterioration that began in the mid-1970s continued throughout the 1980s as a result of the government's failure to implement the necessary policies to correct growing imbalances and adverse international conditions. GDP declined by 16 percent in 1982–1983, and, by the end of the decade, the volume of output and exports was 20 percent below that achieved in the mid-1970s. The country's infrastructure and productive assets were in a state of disrepair, and health and nutrition standards had fallen sharply.

The economy was characterized by huge payments imbalances. The fiscal deficit increased from 41 percent of GDP in 1981 to 47 percent in 1989, and the current account deficit widened from 15 percent of GDP in 1981 to 48 percent in 1989. These deficits were mainly financed through increases in the money supply and the buildup of arrears on debt service payments. In 1985, Guyana was declared ineligible for IMF loans, and, by the end of 1988, the external debt was U.S. $1,764 million (including arrears of $1,038 million). This was more than six times the level of exports, and the debt service ratio was 89 percent.

In 1988, the government began negotiations with the IMF and the World Bank over a medium-term Economic Recovery Program. In July 1988, the World Bank, as chair of the Caribbean Group for Cooperation in Economic Development, began the process of mobilizing the $1.9 billion needed to implement the program, including $1.2 billion that was eligible for debt rescheduling. The financing gap of $700 million included $400 million for balance-of-payments support; of this, $180 million was needed to clear arrears to the IMF ($120 million), to the World Bank ($36 million), and to the CDB ($24 million). To fill the gap, a support group chaired by Canada was formed and another financing tour, led by Canada with IMF and World Bank participation, was undertaken in December 1988.

The financing package was not finalized in 1989, and, without any external assistance to cushion the program, Guyana undertook a number of drastic adjustment measures, including devaluation of the exchange rate from G $10 to G $33 per U.S. dollar (passing the increases to retail prices), increases in interest rates, curbs on credit and wage increases, price decontrols, and the sale of government assets. The impact of the program was particularly hard on the poor and the vulnerable, who were already suffering from years of economic decline. Migration continued at the rate of 1,000–2,000 a month, and about half of the jobs in the public sector remained unfilled.

With the help of the support group, Guyana cleared the arrears to the IFIs in June 1990; a month later, the IMF approved a one-year standby arrangement (SDR 49.5 million) and a three-year enhanced structural adjustment facility loan (SDR 81.5 million). This was the first time that arrears to the fund had been settled through this type of collaborative effort by bilateral and multilateral agencies. Arrears to the World Bank ($55.3 million) and to the CDB ($30 million) were also settled, and a few months later, the World Bank group approved a structural adjustment credit of SDR 59.8 million on IDA terms, and the CDB approved a loan of $42 million, also on concessional terms, to be disbursed in conjunction with the IDA credit.

A further fall in output of over 10 percent was registered over 1988–1990; agricultural production was hampered by heavy rains and strikes, and bauxite production was constrained by the lack of inputs and equipment. The government, however, held fast to implementing the adjustment program and the shifts toward a market-oriented economy. A management agreement was signed with a British firm for the sugar industry, joint ventures were concluded for rice and bauxite, and the assets of several state agencies were sold. The fiscal deficit remained large at 55 percent of GDP, and the gap between the official and the parallel exchange rate was still wide, despite successive devaluations. The overall balance-of-payments deficit reached an annual average of U.S. $188 million in

1989–1990 and was financed through Paris Club debt reschedul-
ings and by balance-of-payments support from the IFIs and the
support group.

The economy is beginning to show signs of recovery. GDP has
grown at around 6 percent per annum since 1991. Inflation is
down, and the exchange rate appears to have stabilized, but the
external debt and debt service payments remain large. Total public debt was U.S. $1.9 billion at the end of 1992, more than nine
times the export total; outstanding medium- and long-term debt
was $1.2 billion, of which $539 million was owed to the multilateral agencies, and the short-term foreign liabilities of the Bank of
Guyana amounted to $786 million. Debt to the IMF amounted to
$165 million in 1993, equivalent to 54 percent of projected exports,
and the debt service to other multilateral institutions was U.S. $51
million. In May 1993, the Paris Club rescheduled Guyana's debt
obligations for 1993 and 1994, but this still leaves the debt service
ratio at 50 percent and the total debt at over seven times the volume of exports. Guyana needs a major restructuring of the total
stock of the debt outstanding and large inflows of concessional
assistance over the medium term.

Guyana has not been a major borrower from the CDB. Between
1970 and March 1990, net approvals amounted to $39.76 million,
$15.4 million of which were drawings under the USAID-financed
Caribbean Development Facility. Two-thirds of the CDB's lending
(excluding the CDF) was to the agricultural sector, and no loans
were made after 1982 due to the accumulation of arrears on the
Guyana portfolio that adversely affected the CDB's profitability.

By the end of 1988, overall arrears owed to the CDB amounted
to $34.4 million, of which Guyana accounted for $22.2 million. Net
income from loans declined as a result of the policy on the nonaccrual of interest on loans in arrears for over twelve months and the
provisioning against the principal amounts overdue. At the end of
1988, loan loss provisions amounted to $18.2 million and the
CDB's reserves-to-loans ratio hovered around 25 percent, compared with the internal target of 30 percent. The CDB maintained
a comfortable liquidity position equivalent to two years of projected disbursements, and there was no danger of the bank being
unable to service its borrowings outstanding. However, the arrears
problem limited the bank's ability to borrow on the international
capital markets and reduced its lending capacity. The success of
the support group in resolving the arrears problem of Guyana was
therefore of critical importance to the CDB. The Economic

Recovery Program for Guyana was formulated by the World Bank and the IMF, and most of the policy discussions were conducted by the Washington-based institutions. The CDB participated in the preparation of the PSIP and in monitoring the program's implementation, and in May 1990, the CDB made the largest loan in the bank's history ($42 million) in support of the ERP.

Jamaica (Population 2.4 Million; 1990 Average Per Capita Income $1,290)

During the 1960s, Jamaica experienced GDP growth rates of 5 percent per annum in response to a steady expansion in investment in bauxite and tourism. This growth came to an abrupt halt after the global shocks of 1972–1974, and the rest of the decade was a period of contraction in which GDP declined by 3 percent per annum and unemployment increased to 28 percent of the work force. In 1980, real GDP was 18 percent below the level in 1973. Bauxite, which had been the leading growth sector, declined due to the international recession, and manufacturing output fell by 31 percent due to lack of imported inputs, labor unrest, shortages of skilled labor, and a loss of investor confidence.

The economic crisis that unfolded in Jamaica in the mid-1970s presented a major challenge to the Washington-based development agencies: the IMF, the World Bank, the Inter-American Development Bank, and the USAID. As the situation worsened, it became clear that no single agency could provide the level of resources required by Jamaica without infringing its guidelines on prudent levels of exposure. What seemed important, also, was the establishment of a mechanism to coordinate the advice and financial support of the multilateral and bilateral agencies that Jamaica required. This came into existence when the Caribbean Group for Cooperation in Economic Development was created in 1978.

The CGCED brought together the traditional donors, as well as new sources of assistance, to review the economic policies and programs of the English-speaking Caribbean states and territories, as well as Haiti and the Dominican Republic. A major effort was concentrated on Jamaica. This was, in part, a reflection of its comparative needs, but, at the same time, it seemed to indicate a belief that Jamaica was a country with which an effective dialogue was possible and where the World Bank's evolving doctrine of structural adjustment would eventually bear fruit.

The general framework adopted by the Washington-based

agencies in formulating a program for the process of adjustment in Jamaica involved short-term policies aimed at altering relative prices and the promotion of longer-term structural reforms. These policies have been intended to contain the growth of external indebtedness and to improve the capacity of the economy to service its existing stock of debt as well as prudent levels of new debts.

A 47.6 percent devaluation of the Jamaican dollar in January 1978, followed by the unification in May 1978 of the previous two-tier exchange rate, paved the way for a three-year Extended Fund Facility (EFF) arrangement with the IMF. The conditions attached to the EFF included a package of comprehensive reforms, including the phasing out of price controls and subsidies, the imposition of a ceiling on wage increases, and an improved fiscal effort involving tax increases and curtailment of budgetary expenditures. Performance under the EFF was mixed, and purchases were suspended in September 1979. After an unsuccessful attempt to salvage the program, negotiations were broken off in March 1980.

The government that came to power under Prime Minister Edward Seaga later in 1980 adopted an IMF/World Bank stabilization and adjustment program to reduce public spending and to give a larger role to the private sector in the economy. In support of the program, Jamaica received large amounts of assistance from multilateral and bilateral donors. Between 1981 and 1985, the IMF committed SDR 785.7 million, the World Bank provided $191.4 million, and USAID $503 million under various programs. But during this period GDP grew at only 0.8 percent per annum, largely because of the fall in the price of bauxite—export receipts from bauxite dropped from $648 million in 1980 to $290 million in 1985. The fiscal imbalance remained large, the debt rose to $3.8 billion in 1985, and the unemployment rate stayed close to 25 percent.

The economy began to show signs of recovery in 1987, mainly as a result of improvements in the external sector. Bauxite prices stabilized, oil prices and interest rates fell, and earnings from tourism increased, resulting in a GDP growth of 6 percent in 1987. Output growth fell again to 1.6 percent in 1988, due to the destruction caused by Hurricane Gilbert, and it has since averaged 3 percent per annum. Jamaica is continuing to implement a stringent adjustment program to reduce inflation and the budget deficit, remove distortions, and liberalize trade and capital markets.

The medium-term prospects for the economy are mixed. The outlook for bauxite and agricultural exports is uncertain, but tourism has recently shown strong growth. The movement towards exchange rate and price stability suggests that Jamaica should soon begin to see the benefits of the painful adjustment measures undertaken for more than a decade. But the heavy debt burden remains an obstacle to sustained growth: debt outstanding was $4.2 billion at the end of 1991. Currently, 50 percent of Jamaica's medium- and long-term debt is owed to official bilateral creditors, while multilateral creditors account for approximately 40 percent of that debt. Payments to the IFIs account for 50 percent of total debt service and, under current guidelines, cannot be renegotiated. The World Bank has reached its risk exposure limits in lending to Jamaica. At the end of 1991, its share in Jamaica's multilateral long-term debt, including IMF borrowings, was 16 percent, and the share in total debt (including short-term) was 15 percent. In the light of this level of exposure, the World Bank is pursuing a strategy of seeking to limit the number and relative size of its loans and to help the government to maintain a net flow of resources through cofinancing of World Bank operations with other donors.

The World Bank's country-assistance strategy for Jamaica has been designed to support the objectives and policies expressed in the government's Medium-Term Policy Framework Paper for the period 1992/93 to 1994/95. This document commits the Jamaican government to the reshaping of the public sector in order to nurture an economy in which the private sector is dominant. Thus, the World Bank's lending strategy will emphasize support for the completion of further reforms in the areas of privatization, deregulation, and the trade regime. The World Bank intends, also, to finance sector investment loans designed to support Jamaica's efforts to liberalize the economy, privatize public enterprises, and improve competitiveness.

The situation noted above suggests that Jamaica will have to depend on the IDB as its major source of multilateral development finance in the future. The IDB's seventh replenishment of its resources provided it with the capacity to lend some U.S. $22 billion to its borrowing members for 1990–1993. It has programmed U.S. $550 million in loans to Jamaica, and, under present terms, Jamaica's debt outstanding to the IDB could reach U.S. $800 to $900 million by 1995. This would mean that the IDB's share of Jamaica's debt outstanding to the MDBs would increase to 60 percent of the total. The IDB is using its seventh replenishment mandate to become involved in policy-based lending to Jamaica to finance sectoral reforms aimed at bringing about structural transformation, while continuing to pursue its traditional role of lending for specific projects in social and economic infrastructure. However, the IDB has taken note of the World Bank's experience and plans to pursue a cautious policy of closely tying disbursements of its loans to the capacity of the Jamaican government to implement the envisioned reforms.

Jamaica's preoccupation with negotiating financial assistance from the Washington-based IFIs in support of its adjustment efforts may well have detracted from its capacity to make a significant contribution to the governance of the CDB. Jamaica has been represented on the CDB's Board of Directors in recent times by second-line officials in the ministry of finance. Even when account is taken of the limited number of management posts on the CDB's staff, that representation by Jamaica has not been significant.[2]

In turn, the CDB's influence on what was a central policy concern for Jamaica has been slight. Although the CDB participated as a donor in the CGCED, from its inception it does not appear to have played a significant role in the development of a common view by the donor community on the design and implementation of programs of stabilization and structural adjustment in the small, highly open Caribbean economies.[3] Perhaps the main reason for this reticence was not so much that the CDB did not have the financial resources to make a major contribution to Jamaica's resource requirements, but that it was slow to perceive the importance of developing its own position on the structural adjustment issue and did not do so until the second half of the 1980s. This may have been the result of the Bank's staff limitations in the areas of macroeconomic and sector work, reflecting its initial emphasis as an agency for financing public sector projects.

The CDB has provided Jamaica with limited amounts of project financing during the past two decades, but it cannot be said that the portfolio of investments to which these resources have been allocated has been based on a continuing and consistent country assistance strategy. A major peculiarity of the Jamaica portfolio is that it is heavily skewed in favor of development finance operations.

The CDB has put considerable resources into strengthening the National Development Bank (NDB) and the Agricultural Credit Bank (ACB), the two second-story institutions through which the loans have been disbursed. The ACB was established in 1982, and it on-lends through a network of approved financial institutions (AFIs), including commercial banks, private development banks, and cooperative banks. The NDB was established in 1983 and makes loans to the manufacturing, tourism, mining, and services sectors through seventeen approved financial institutions. The CDB has provided the ACB and NDB with 30–40 percent of their resources, and this has proven to be a cost-effective means of supporting the development of the private sector. The responsibility for disbursement rests with the AFIs, which appraise the applications of subborrowers, obtain funds from ACB and NDB, and bear the credit risks.

An evaluation report by independent consultants concluded that the ACB and NDB have made significant contributions to the economy through increases in output, exports, and employment. The rate of return on subprojects ranged from 14–19 percent, and less than 1 percent of their loan portfolios was classified as bad debts. Much of the investment in agriculture between 1985 and 1990 has been in export crops and would not have taken place without the benefit of subsidized credit.[4] Since 1990, the ACB has had to increase its interest rate in keeping with the World Bank/IDB agricultural sector loan, and this has resulted in a decline in demand for its loans. The CDB has taken issue with the World Bank and the IDB on this matter and has suggested that these high interest rates will adversely affect small farmers and are inconsistent with long-term growth objectives.

The CDB staff has suggested that the focus on credit projects has been appropriate: the investment in agriculture between 1985 and 1990 was essentially in crops, which had benefited from export niches, and would not otherwise have taken place without the benefit of subsidized credit. Tourism projects had used the access to credit to expand investment and increase foreign exchange earnings. The CDB staff argued, also, that the manufacturing sector would be able to export competitively only if foreign exchange were available for retooling.

Jamaican officials have expressed concern over the absence of a significant pipeline of projects with the CDB. They have pointed out that there is only one new project for which financing is being considered—in rural electrification—and suggested that the CDB could be more proactive in identifying opportunities. This may be an area of some contention, because the CDB's management has suggested that the discussions that they have had with the Jamaican authorities revealed that the projects presented had rates of return that were too low to meet the CDB's selection criteria.

The concerns expressed by the Jamaican authorities over the weakness of their pipeline with the CDB suggests that there is an underlying weakness in the Bank's country-assistance planning. It is to be noted that other MDBs prepare country briefs that provide executive directors and senior management with up-to-date information on their active borrowing countries. These briefs usually summarize the country's recent policy performance, its main development constraints, its economic objectives, and macro-economic prospects and outline the bank's role, strategy, and lending operations. In the preparation of these briefs, careful attention is paid to detailing the MDB's objectives, strategy, overall lending program, and assessment of risks, together with the country's debt and debt service obligations to the bank.

There seems to be clear justification for a greater degree of transparency by the CDB's management in its country-assistance planning. The Jamaican authorities have suggested that the CDB appears to have adopted a policy of restricting its risk exposure in lending to their country. It would be desirable, therefore, for the CDB's management to seek guidance on what actions might be appropriate to avoid a significant reduction of its presence and a possible deterioration of its portfolio in Jamaica.

It is difficult for the CDB to plan an effective program of future assistance to Jamaica that makes efficient use of its limited resources in the absence of an assessment of its past operations. To date, because the CDB's capacity for operations evaluation is extremely limited, only two of the twenty-three projects for which loans have been fully disbursed have been the subject of performance assessment by the Post-Implementation and Evaluation Unit for Jamaica (other than the recent evaluation of loans to ACB and NDB). In planning a strategy for future lending to Jamaica, which will probably come mainly from special fund resources, the CDB should undertake a complete country assessment and project performance review.

Jamaica's need for balance-of-payments support over the past two decades greatly exceeded the CDB's capacity to lend, and, as has been noted, the Bank had no role to play in the policy discussions that have been led by the World Bank, the IMF, and IDB. But the CDB has carved out a niche for itself in financing small- to medium-scale enterprises in the productive sector and in capital market development. The project portfolio has suffered recently from disbursement problems due to the fall in the demand for credit, rising costs, and budget cuts limiting the availability of counterpart financing. Future lending will be constrained by the large undisbursed balance and Jamaica's share of the loan portfolio.

It is clear that the CDB's impact on the development process in

Jamaica over the past two decades has been limited. During this period Jamaica has been involved in an intensive dialogue with the Washington-based IFIs on the design and implementation of an appropriate program of stabilization and structural adjustment. While the CDB has not been centrally involved in these discussions, there is a certain body of evidence that its technical staff have been, at least, skeptical about the prescriptions that have been pressed on Jamaica.

A key issue remains the overall appropriateness of the structural adjustment program (SAP). As one former CDB economist has noted, the most glaring feature of the SAP is the emphasis placed on the market mechanism to allocate resources efficiently in factor, product, credit, and foreign exchange markets. Thus, the theory of the "second best" suggests that selective interventions in the functioning of markets may be superior to the liberalization policies advocated in some cases.

In the area of trade liberalization, Jamaica has been the standard bearer in efforts promoted by the World Bank to lower the average incidence of the Common External Tariff (CET) and roll back quantitative restrictions. Many of the CARICOM countries tend to view the trade liberalization process with suspicion. They have been concerned that the complete removal of quota restrictions and the lowering of tariff rates will result in import growth and reserve losses during the transition period.

It is important for the CDB to take a definitive position on this matter since its Articles of Agreement give it a mandate to assist regional members to coordinate the expansion of their trade. Since the collapse of the CARICOM Multilateral Clearing Facility, intraregional trade has been hampered by the absence of an appropriate clearance mechanism. This may be an area to which the CDB could devote some attention.

A review of CDB's relations with Jamaica casts doubt on the assumption that the larger borrowing member countries are likely to require less direct involvement by the Bank in the development of programs of external assistance and the establishment of priorities among the projects to which that assistance should be directed. While the Bank has been justified in focusing on the needs of its smaller members, the economic crisis of the 1970s and 1980s has severely depleted the technical resources of its larger borrowing members, who are now likely to demand a greater degree of attention from the Caribbean Development Bank as their access to alternative sources of financing declines. The decisions of the nonregional members of the CDB in supporting an increase in the resources of the Bank will be crucial to enhancing the contribution that the CDB can make to the problems of adjustment and growth in Jamaica.

Notes

1. The Organization of Eastern Caribbean States (OECS) include Antigua and Barbuda, Dominica, Grenada, St. Kitts-Nevis, St. Lucia, Montserrat, and St. Vincent and the Grenadines.

2. Jamaica seems to have a strong claim to the position of vice-president of corporate affairs and secretary, much in keeping with the type of informal arrangement in regional development banks under which particular management positions are allocated to specific countries.

3. It is interesting to note that at the CDB's annual meeting of the Board of Governors, in 1980, the governor for Jamaica attempted to bring the CDB into the debate on the design and implementation of an appropriate stabilization program by making a lengthy presentation on the state of negotiations in his country. With the change in administration that took place in Jamaica later that year, Edward Seaga, the prime minister and minister of finance, assumed the position of governor for Jamaica on the CDB. However, although he was actively involved in all areas of economic policy formulation and negotiation with funding agencies, his schedule prevented his participation in CDB's annual meetings of the Board of Governors.

4. This conclusion is confirmed by a World Bank project evaluation report, which notes that discussions with subborrowers suggest that, in spite of the existence of noninterest rate incentives, investment would have been considerably lower without the "cheap credit" provided under the project ("Jamaica: Export Crops Project," World Bank, Report no. 10656, p. 11).

PART 2

DEVELOPMENT AGENDA

6

RESOURCE MOBILIZATION

In 1992 the CDB received a triple-A rating from Moody's Investors Service. In making the announcement, Moody's stated that "the rating is based on the strong capital structure of the bank and on its preferred creditor status with borrowing countries, as well as on its financial policies that minimize risk while achieving adequate profitability. Another important factor is the support of five triple-A rated members."[1] The agency also noted that the CDB had the second most favorable risk ratio among the rated development banks. The CDB is the first financial institution in the Caribbean to be given a triple-A rating, and this is a reflection of its sound management and prudent financial policies over the past two decades.

The CDB's financial resources consist of ordinary capital resources that include authorized capital, borrowed funds, loan repayments, and accumulated net income; and of special fund resources (SFR) that consist of contributed funds, repayments, and income from SFR operations. The Venezuelan Trust Fund (VTF) was established in 1975 with a contribution of $25 million from the government of Venezuela, which has the right to the return of all loan repayments and net income earned. At the end of 1992, the total resources available for lending amounted to $985 million (see Table 6.1).

Ordinary Capital Resources (OCR)

During the 1970s, OCR resources grew rapidly with the expansion of the Bank's capital base and borrowing. Over the decade, there were three capital increases that raised the authorized and subscribed capital from $50 million in 1970 to $282 million in 1979. The CDB was able to borrow the equivalent of $72.05 million—from

Table 6.1   Total Resources: 1970–1992 (in millions of dollars)

Year	OCR	VTF	SFR	Total
1970	5.4	—	—	5.4
1980	132.4	25.0	238.5	395.9
1985	190.0	14.8	375.3	580.1
1986	192.7	13.1	392.1	597.9
1987	197.3	12.0	424.0	633.3
1988	210.0	11.0	511.7	732.7
1989	219.6	10.3	541.6	771.5
1990	264.5	9.3	589.4	863.2
1991	308.1	8.5	573.9	890.5
1992	335.9	7.7	641.1	984.7

Source: CDB Annual Report, various years.

the World Bank ($43 million), regional central banks ($9.75 million), Trinidad and Tobago ($15 million), and the European Investment Bank ($4.3 million). By contrast, during the 1980s there was no general capital increase and no borrowing and OCR resources grew at a snail's pace, except that the admission to membership of France, Italy, and Germany (1984, 1988, and 1989 respectively), coupled with the accompanying increase in the shareholdings of Commonwealth Caribbean Members in order to maintain a majority of the shareholdings, resulted in an increase in subscribed capital from $282 million in 1979 to $448.4 million in 1989.

The Bank operates under very strict guidelines, set by the Board of Directors, that limit the level of borrowing and lending. The ceiling on borrowing is equal to the callable capital of the OECD members, and in 1987 the amount of borrowed funds was 89 percent of the ceiling. After Italy and Germany became members in 1988 and 1989, the limit on borrowing increased to $152 million and was further raised to $215 million after the capital increase in 1991. This expansion of the capital base enabled the CDB to borrow $20 million from the World Bank in 1990 and $30 million from the U.S. private placement market in 1992. At the end of 1992, net OCR borrowings amounted to $94.8 million—less than half of the ceiling and only 10 percent of total resources.

Special Fund Resources (SFR)

SFR consist of the Unified Special Development Fund (USDF), which consists of contributions from CDB's members and the

Netherlands; other special development funds (OSDF), which are contributions and concessional loans by members and nonmembers; and other special funds (OSF), which are concessionary resources contributed by members, nonmembers, and international financial institutions. Contributions have come from a large number of countries including the United States, United Kingdom, Canada, Venezuela, Germany, Italy, Colombia, Nigeria, Sweden, Trinidad, and the Netherlands, and from IDB, EDF, and IDA. In 1991 replenishment negotiations for the Unified SDF were completed, and donors committed $124 million to fund programs over 1992–1995. (See Table 6.2.)

Table 6.2   Special Fund Resources: 1991 and 1992 (in millions of dollars)

	1991	1992
United Special Development Fund	287.9	302.2
Other Special Development Fund	98.1	94.0
Total SDF	386.0	396.2
Other Special Funds	173.0	179.9
Total Special Fund Resources	559.0	576.1

Source: CDB.

Special fund resources account for two-thirds of the Bank's resources and are a very important component of its operations. These funds have specific rules for procurement and use, which are negotiated with the donors. In general, the funds are used to finance high-priority projects that are not self-liquidating or that have low financial rates of return. Most SFR loans have gone to the LDCs, but there is now a growing tendency to blend OCR and SFR in loans to eligible borrowers.

During the 1980s, the CDB's operations were constrained by the payments problems of several borrowers, which resulted in considerable delays in project implementation. The high level of loan cancellations in 1984 and the drop in approvals in 1985 occurred because several borrowers were unable to meet their share of project costs. (See Table 6.3.)

Lending operations were also curtailed by the shortage of loanable funds. The cancellations in 1986 were initiated by the CDB to close slow-disbursing loans and free resources for new loans, but OCR loan approvals were only $12.5 million per annum in 1987 and 1988 (a quarter of total lending). The ceiling on

Table 6.3   Annual Loan Approvals (in millions of dollars)

	OCR	SFR	Cancellation	Net
1984	17.3	43.9	14.4	46.8
1985	22.8	19.0	8.5	33.3
1986	24.2	35.8	22.2	37.8
1987	12.0	28.1	4.3	35.8
1988	13.0	52.9	0.3	65.6
1989	43.5	32.0	2.4	73.1
1990	51.0	63.7	14.2	100.5
1991	75.3	32.9	0.3	107.9

Source: CDB Annual Report, various years.

lending is the sum of the paid-in capital, ordinary reserves, and the callable capital of the OECD members. In 1988, the CDB was at 76 percent of the OCR lending limit and did not actively promote new lending until the squeeze on resources was removed with the expansion in membership in 1988/1989 and the clearance of Guyana's arrears in 1990.

In the 1980s, the CDB had to face fairly widespread arrears on its loans. However, by refusing to approve new loans or disburse on existing loans, a buildup of protracted arrears was avoided, except in Guyana and Antigua and Barbuda. Total arrears amounted to $34 million in 1988, with Guyana accounting for $22 million and Antigua and Barbuda for $4.3 million. In 1988, the amount of nonperforming loans reached $60.4 million, or 15 percent of the overall portfolio;[2] loan loss provisions totalled $18.2 million, which exceeded OCR loan approvals in 1987–1988 by 50 percent. The arrears of Antigua and Barbuda were reduced in 1989, and Guyana's arrears were cleared in 1990.

As of July 1992, total arrears were $25 million, of which the loans in accrual status amounted to $11 million (3 percent of total loans outstanding). The loans in arrears included two public sector loans to Antigua and Barbuda ($5.8 million), a regional loan ($8 million), and seven private sector loans. All the loans have been called except for the loans to Antigua and Barbuda, and the CDB will receive the proceeds from the sale of the assets of the West Indian Shipping Corporation (WISCO), and four hotels. The WISCO shareholders have agreed to service the EU loan to the CDB that was on-lent to WISCO, and discussions are continuing with Antigua and Barbuda.

Net income dropped sharply from an average of $3.5 million in 1981–1983 to $1.6 million in 1984 as a result of the policy on the nonaccrual of interest on loans in arrears for more than twelve months. In 1986, OCR net income dropped to $0.9 million due to provisioning against the principal amounts overdue. In 1987, the Board of Directors approved a number of measures to strengthen the Bank's financial position; these included the paying of shareholders' maintenance-of-value obligations, encashing noninterest-bearing demand notes held as part of the paid-in capital of some shareholders, and seeking a general capital increase. The implementation of these measures by 1990 significantly improved the CDB's profitability as is illustrated in Table 6.4.

Table 6.4   CDB Profitability Ratios

	1987	1988	1989	1990	1991
Net income (in millions of dollars)	4.1	6.5	6.9	25.9a	12.4
Return on assets (percent)	2.0	3.6	3.5	11.5	4.9
Interest coverageb	1.6	2.2	2.3	6.0	3.6

Source: CDB.
Notes: a. This increase reflected the settlement of Guyana's arrears against which the CDB had been making annual provisions.
b. Interest coverage measures the ability of the borrower to pay interest payments from current available resources. Here the number indicates by what margin the net income of the CDB exceeded interest payment obligations.

Liquidity levels indicate the availability of funds to meet cashflow commitments, and the CDB has maintained a steady growth of liquidity in relation to the growth of debt and assets even during the difficult period in the mid-1980s. In 1991 the ratio of liquid assets to undisbursed loans and projected debt service was 52.4 percent; and the steady increase in the ratio of liquid assets to total debt is both a reflection of higher levels of liquidity and low debt. The ratios show a comfortable level of liquidity, and earnings from the investment portfolio account for 23.4 percent of total income—another indicator of sound financial management. (See Table 6.5.)

The CDB's loan portfolio is highly concentrated among a handful of borrowers, which is not surprising given its size. Three-quarters of the loan portfolio is held by five countries: Jamaica (30.2 percent), Barbados (14.8 percent), Cayman Islands (12.2 percent), Trinidad and Tobago (9 percent), and the Bahamas (8.8 percent); these countries also account for 85 percent of the region's GDP. Overall, the country distribution of loans falls within the

Table 6.5   CDB Liquidity Ratios (percent)

	1987	1988	1989	1990	1991
Liquid assets/undisbursed					
loans and debt service	46.2	66.0	50.5	73.1	52.4
Liquid assets/debt	34.1	44.4	46.1	59.9	65.1
Liquid/total assets	15.8	17.3	15.5	22.0	20.3

Source: CDB.

Bank's established exposure limits. The OCR exposure for Jamaica was 40 percent of net worth at the end of 1991 compared with the maximum exposure for one country of 50 percent, and the OCR exposure in Jamaica, Barbados, and the Cayman Islands was 85 percent of net worth compared with the maximum limit of 100 percent for the three largest borrowers.

The project quality of the portfolio is generally good. In 1991, the loan portfolio contained 542 loans, and the average status of all loans was 1.56 (on a scale of one = no problem to three = major problems). The projects department recently carried out a review of 105 projects under implementation, which showed that seventy-one projects had minor to no problems, twenty-six had moderate problems, eight had major problems, and the overall portfolio performance index was 74.2.[3]

The emphasis on infrastructure, which accounts for 40 percent of the Bank's total lending, was necessary to support the expansion of exports and the growth of tourism. Despite the economic difficulties of the borrowers, cost overruns for infrastructure projects were not large, and implementation was reasonably on schedule. A number of productive sector projects experienced financial, managerial, and technical difficulties that required additional technical assistance to the DFCs and increased supervision. A few projects (notably livestock, fisheries, and land settlement projects) have not been successful, and the postimplementation reports suggest that the fault was in the design and in shifting government priorities in the agricultural sector. To improve the quality of the loan portfolio, the CDB intends to pay greater attention to the design of projects, to increase supervision, and to stress improved project management, marketing, and institution-building.

The CDB has had a successful track record in mobilizing resources and is well placed to play a much larger role in financing development in the region. Since 1970, the Bank has approved loans totalling $1 billion, disbursed $700 million, and financed about 6 percent of the public sector investment programs of the region; in some of the smaller countries, the Bank has financed 30-40 percent of public sector investment. The CDB's borrowers are heavily reliant on external resource flows to finance investment, and the prospects for increased capital flows are not good. The IDA has graduated Antigua and Barbuda and St. Kitts-Nevis. The World Bank has graduated the Bahamas and Barbados, but the decision to graduate Trinidad and Tobago has been reversed for the time being due to the recent decline in its per capita income. Commercial bank lending to the region has dried up and would, in any case, worsen the debt problem of member countries. Finally, bilateral donors are confronted with reduced aid budgets.

However, the CDB's ability to increase the level of lending is constrained by the small size of its capital stock, which is only 1 percent of the IDB's. At the end of 1991, OCR loan approvals amounted to $302 million, or 83 percent of the OCR lending limit, and a significant capital increase is needed to enable the CDB to increase the level of lending and finance a larger share of PSIPs in the region. Since 1970, the CDB has had six capital increases, three associated with the expansion of its members and three general capital increases. The last GCI was in 1991 and brought the total subscribed capital to $648 million (see Table 6.6).

Table 6.6   Trends in Capitalization of the CDB

Year	Subscribed (millions of dollars)	Increase (percent)	Paid-in (percent)	Reason
1970	50.0		50.0	
1972	108.6	117.2	50.0	Membership
1974	192.0	76.8	50.0	GCI
1979	281.6	46.7	18.3	GCI
1985	347.0	23.2	23.1	Membership
1988	448.4	29.2	23.1	Membership
1991	648.0	44.5	22.1	GCI

Source: CDB.

In June 1992, the CDB estimated the capital requirements of its borrowers at $689 million for 1992–1995 after all other sources were taken into account; it could provide less than half of this amount. The proposed OCR lending program for 1992–1995 was $288 million, and the CDB could have some difficulty in meeting these planned lending targets due to limits on its commitment authority. The OCR resources available are not enough for the CDB to lend to the more creditworthy borrowers or to blend with concessional resources, and OCR lending could fall to one-third of total lending by 1995. To maintain OCR lending at the current level of about $55 million per annum, a 50 percent capital increase ($300 million) is needed with 15 percent paid-in; to increase OCR lending to $75 million per annum, a 100 percent GCI is needed.[4]

The need of borrowers and the reduction in alternative sources of development assistance is only part of the argument for a large capital increase. Of equal significance is the fact that the CDB has proven itself to be a well managed bank and a cost-effective means of resource transfer. Its financial ratios compare well with those of the larger multilateral development banks in terms of profitability, liquidity, and quality of the loan portfolio; its net income is growing, and it enjoys a high credit rating. But the CDB is poorly capitalized in relation to the other MDBs operating in the region and in its capacity to make good loans. This constraint should be removed to enable the Bank to build on its achievements and expand its lending operations. (See Table 6.7.)

Table 6.7   Selected Financial Indicators

	1988	1989	1990	1991	1992
Reserves-to-loans (percent) (min. 30 percent)	28.5	31.6	46.9	51.6	55.3
Borrowings as percent of borrowing capacity	61.0	45.0	58.0	37.0	44.0
OCR loan commitment as percent of lending limit	76.0	77.0	79.0	76.0	78.0
Long-term debt/equity (ratio)	0.55	0.50	0.41	0.32	0.36

Source: CDB.

In addition to seeking a significant capital increase, the CDB should vigorously pursue expanded membership. Commitment authority would increase by $125 million if the United States and Japan both became members, and each new EU member would contribute an additional $37.5 million. Commonwealth Caribbean members would have to increase their own capital subscriptions by as much as any new member in order to retain majority ownership. This would undoubtedly create difficulties, given the severity of their current balance-of-payments problems, but a number of options can be considered to ease the burden, including payments in local currencies and protracted payment arrangements.

Notes

1. Press release, *DCB News*, September 1992.
2. OCR nonperforming loans amounted to 21.2 percent of the OCR loan portfolio, and this impaired CDB's willingness to attempt to borrow on the international capital markets.
3. Status of CDB projects under implementation as of March 31, 1994.
4. In July 1994 the CDB Executive Board adopted a resolution that may make a general capital increase unnecessary for the next three years. The Board decided to interpret the "lending level" as "loans outstanding and disbursed" rather than the OCR loan commitment level. Because disbursements always lag behind commitments, this will allow the commitment level to rise to 133 percent of the statutory limit (OECD capital subscriptions) before the new ceiling (disbursements equal to 100 percent of OECD capital) is reached. At that point, a new general capital increase should be considered.

7

Development
Agency Functions

In addition to lending for investment, the CDB is required by its Charter to undertake other functions of a development agency including the provision of technical assistance, economic support and analysis, and the promotion of regional economic cooperation and integration. Over the past two decades, the main activity has been the provision of technical assistance grants and soft loans of almost $100 million, or 10 percent of total lending. The Bank has also undertaken economic analysis and policy coordination, particularly for the smaller member countries, and financed regional projects and studies.

Technical Assistance

Article 2 of the Charter requires the CDB "to provide appropriate technical assistance to its regional members, particularly by undertaking or commissioning pre-investment surveys and by assisting in the identification and preparation of project proposals." From the beginning, the provision of technical assistance was seen as one of the primary functions of the Bank. The 1972 annual report noted that it was "a matter of semantics whether the institution is regarded as a technical assistance agency which also lends money, or as a Bank which also prepares projects."

During the 1970s, the lack of grant funds limited the scope for providing direct technical assistance. As a result, the staff spent 25–30 percent of their time on project-related activities that would normally be carried out by borrowers and in preparing technical studies, advising governments, and complementing the work of other regional institutions in promoting economic integration. By the end of the decade, it was evident that more resources were needed for technical assistance because several borrowers were having difficulties preparing and implementing projects and were unable to make effective use of the CDB's lending due to institutional and technical constraints.

The Technical Assistance Fund (TAF) was created in 1978 with contributions from the United Kingdom, Canada, Venezuela, Trinidad and Tobago, CDB, USAID, and Mexico, and the fund enabled the CDB to formalize its role in the provision of technical assistance. Two evaluations were carried out in 1980 and 1984 by independent consultants; these helped the Bank to strengthen the operational and administrative aspects of the program by creating the Technical Cooperation Unit to manage all technical assistance and training programs.

Technical assistance grants totaled $70.8 million at the end of 1991, of which 90.6 percent went to the LDCs. The MDCs received only $4.5 million, including the grant of $2 million to Guyana in 1990 in support of the Economic Recovery Program. Resources have been made available for training, advisory services, institutional strengthening, preinvestment activities, project preparation and implementation, and trade promotion. Beneficiaries must make counterpart contributions of at least 15 percent to the project's cost. The CDB also executes regional technical assistance projects funded from outside sources, and bank staff continue to devote roughly 30 percent of their time to supplying indirect technical assistance.

A brief description of some of the more important technical assistance programs follows.

The Caribbean Technological Consultancy Services Network (CTCS) was launched in 1982 with assistance from the International Development Research Centre (IDRC), and it has been in full operation since 1985. The network provides fast and practical responses to requests for assistance and offers a wide range of consultancy services, training, and technical information to small- and medium-scale businesses, particularly in the agro-industry and food processing sectors. The DFCs frequently use CTCS for technical appraisals, marketing studies, and advisory services in support of their loan portfolios.

The CDB operates CTCS with the help of regional and national institutions, development agencies, industrial enterprises, and individual specialists or consulting firms who register with the network. Institutions providing assistance include the Caribbean

Industrial Research Institute, the UWI faculty of engineering, the Caribbean Metal Industries Company, the Jamaica Bureau of Standards, and the Barbados Institute of Management and Productivity. The services offered by CTCS include field visits, training, and information; in some instances, clients visit the establishments of resource persons to learn and practice new skills.

Between 1985 and 1991, the network handled approximately 1,500 requests for assistance, which required 985 weeks of field consultation. CTCS also publishes a newsletter; prepares information packages on technical subjects, industry profiles, and a directory of regional experts; and maintains an extensive database linked to the Bank's library. The network has been financed through contributions from the CDB, UNDP (up to 1985), IDRC (up to 1989), and the nominal fees paid by beneficiaries. The full cost of the network is now being met from fees and contributions from the CDB.

CTCS is a very successful program. In 1989 an evaluation commissioned by IDRC commended its support to the small business sector; the CDB's evaluation in 1991 confirmed this finding and the benefit of the service at the level of personal interaction. The 1991 evaluation drew attention to the shift in the type of expertise required by clients from solutions to basic operational problems to more technical matters such as the development of management systems, preparation of feasibility studies, and computerization. CTCS respond to these new demands while containing operating costs and preserving the underlying objectives of the network.

The objective of the project administration (PA) and national economic management (NEM) training programs is to strengthen economic management in the region through training in project analysis and in the design and implementation of macroeconomic policies. The training is conducted by CDB staff and consultants from national, regional, and international organizations. The 1987 evaluation report noted that the PA program was well conceived and commended its achievements in training over 2,000 persons; however, additional resources are needed to conduct these courses more frequently and to expand coverage to the private sector in order to improve project performance and the efficiency of investments.

The NEM program was started in 1985 by the Economic Development Institute of the World Bank (EDI) and the Latin American Institute of Economic and Social Planning (ILPES). ILPES no longer takes part in the training, and EDI has scaled down its involvement. There is an acute shortage of trained personnel to implement the structural adjustment programs being carried out by Jamaica, Guyana, Trinidad and Tobago, Barbados, and several of the smaller countries; and IDB and the World Bank should provide assistance to the CDB to expand greatly the training programs in macroeconomic management. The CDB has also conducted courses for senior- and middle-level officials in government and regional institutions; it sees a need for more of these courses so that a greater number of public officials can be exposed to training and new thinking on development issues.

The Caribbean Basin Water Management Project (CBWMP) was sponsored by CIDA, PAHO/WHO, the CDB, and thirteen countries: OECS members, Barbados, Belize, British Virgin Islands, Cayman Islands, and Turks and Caicos Islands. The project's objectives were to improve the management and operation of water and sewerage utilities in the region and to foster awareness of the importance of training through the use of indigenous, self-sustaining programs. The project began in 1975 and has been managed by the CDB since 1983. Areas of training include ground water development, preventive maintenance, stores management and inventory control, human resource development, financial management, and the training of trainers. Resource persons are drawn mostly from participating utilities. The 1985 midterm evaluation recognized the project as a unique and outstanding example of successful regional cooperation. In 1991, the CDB handed over the responsibility for the management of the program to the participating public utilities.

Since the mid-1970s, the CDB has made continual efforts to mobilize financial and technical assistance for energy development. The Alternative Energy System Program (AESP) was instituted in 1979 by the CARICOM secretariat, CDB, and USAID. The program included assessments of national energy needs and resources, the formulation of energy policies, the preparation of studies, and adaptive research projects.

The Regional Energy Action Plan (REAP) was formulated in 1983 and implemented at the request of the CARICOM heads of government. The plan was prepared by the CDB and the CARICOM secretariat, with the cooperation of regional governments. REAP's objective was to alleviate the adverse impact of the energy crisis on regional economies and provide a more coordinated and rational approach to the development of regional energy resources. The program focused on energy conservation, power sector development, strengthening national and regional institutions, exploitation of new and renewable sources of energy, and man-power development and training. Despite assistance from the German Agency for Technical Cooperation (GTZ), REAP proceeded slowly due to insufficient financing. The achievements of the CDB/GTZ component, which ended in 1991, have been in energy conservation and the development of new and renewable energy sources.

In future, the CDB plans to integrate the provision of technical assistance more closely with the priorities in the PSIPs and to replace individual applications for technical assistance with a planned two-year program for each country. Priority will be given to human resource development, poverty alleviation, and environmental protection. The current slowdown in disbursements reflects bottlenecks in institutional capacity and the supply of skilled labor. As the CDB moves into new areas of lending and larger projects, increased technical assistance will be needed to enhance absorptive capacity.

Economic Analysis and Policy Coordination

The primary responsibility of the Economics Department, with its staff of six economists, is to support the Bank's lending programs and to provide a liaison with the IFIs and aid donors. Departmental tasks include preparing annual economic reports for seventeen borrowing member countries; preparing public sector investment programs for the OECS countries and U.K. dependencies; providing comments on project briefs and on sectoral policy papers; and producing sections of the Bank's annual report that deal with economic matters.

Each economist is also a member of the country project team and is required to make a preliminary assessment indicating whether the project is included in the PSIP, sectoral constraints, questions that need to be asked during appraisal, and policy conditionality. Economists are also required to carry out special assignments for regional institutions and borrowers, to respond to donor requests for information, and to conduct training programs. The staff are knowledgeable about the borrowers and the issues affecting their development, but they lack the time and resources to carry out in-depth analysis.

Since 1977, the CDB has been participating in the Caribbean Group for Cooperation in Economic Development, the consultative aid group for the region, and the Bank's economics department is responsible for helping to draw up the agenda for the meeting and preparing background papers and aid coordination meetings for the OECS countries and the U.K. dependencies. Based on the success of the Fund for Emergency Program and Common Services in the OECS countries, the CDB proposed to the aid group in 1978 that a similar program for the MDCs be established; as a result, the Caribbean Development Facility (CDF) was created. The CDF provided $65 million between 1979 and 1982 through the CDB to enable the MDCs to implement investment projects.

The volume of economic work carried out for the Caribbean region is large and costly, and there is considerable duplication of effort and responsibility. In addition to the CDB's reports, the World Bank, the IMF, and IDB also produce regular economic reports and conduct special studies. Borrowers attach importance to the reports of the World Bank and the IMF but pay little attention to the reports of the other agencies that tend to go over the same ground. CDB staff have published refereed articles on inflation and money demand and are researching areas such as tourism development and real exchange rate determination. However, in a region of six million people, there is no rationale for all the MDBs to produce annual economic reports and carry out studies on the same issues. These institutions should therefore agree on a division of responsibility and an exchange of information to avoid duplication and to raise the overall quality of economic work and research.

A move towards such a division of labor was made recently in the Memorandum of Understanding concluded between the World Bank and the CDB in 1990. This gives the CDB responsibility for the economic work in the U.K.–dependent territories and for the preparation of PSIPs for the OECS countries, Belize, and the U.K. territories. The World Bank will carry out all economic work on the MDCs and prepare the economic reports on the OECS countries and Belize. However, this agreement only covers the preparation of country economic reports and PSIPs; there is no mechanism for determining what work needs to be done on regional issues and which institution should do it. Despite the involvement of all these agencies, there is a paucity of work on important issues such as the size and characteristics of the informal economy that is very significant in Guyana, Jamaica, and some OECS countries. Other issues that need to be studied are emigration, capital flight, unemployment, and emerging capital markets in the Bahamas, Jamaica, and Barbados; the volume and quality of aid flows; the debt problem, terms of trade, and export prospects; and trends in direct foreign investment, net transfers, and remittances.

The CDB does not have the resources to study these issues, but the Bank should become more involved in influencing what work is done. On the grounds of efficiency and improving the overall quality of the information and analysis, there needs to be an annual consultation between the World Bank, the IDB, and the CDB on the programming of economic work to set priorities and to establish a clear division of labor. Procedures also need to be established for the exchange of information through computer linkages on what studies are being done, and more collaboration is needed between the MDBs in carrying out studies. Most of the responsibility for economic work should be carried out by the larger MDBs, which have large research and statistical departments and the resources to employ specialists. More resources are also needed to enhance the capacity of the OECS and CARICOM secretariats to undertake economic research and analysis.

The CDB needs to carve a role for itself in the area of economic analysis as it has done in project lending. It should avoid limited coverage of a large number of issues and instead should build up expertise by undertaking in-depth analysis of fewer issues; it could commission and collaborate on work in other areas. There is a wealth of talent in the region that the CDB could tap for economic analysis and policy coordination; this was shown in the team put together and led by the CDB to prepare the medium-term adjustment program for Grenada. The CDB needs to take an intellectual leadership role in highlighting important issues affecting the region's development. For example, all the MDBs are emphasizing increased lending for human resource development and educational reform, but there is very little analysis of future manpower needs and the impact of emigration from the region. It may make sense for the Caribbean to educate people for export to the North, but this should be a clearly defined policy with remittance and other benefits. The CDB should serve as a catalyst to identify research priorities and to commission studies. The Bank should look for support from governments, the MDBs, and UN organizations in hosting symposiums on regional development issues.

Should the CDB become more involved in the design of policy-based lending, as many borrowers have suggested? It cannot compete in this area with the IMF, World Bank, and the IDB, which have at their disposal hundreds of economists and specialist staff, but the CDB can contribute its knowledge of the region, the policymakers, and the people who have to implement these programs.

It should also be more closely involved in the regional policy for-
mulations of the Washington institutions.

Regional Cooperation

The countries of the Caribbean have strong cultural ties that derive
from their common history and geography. However, they have
few economic linkages due to their small size, identical production
structures, and lack of low-cost transportation. The CDB has
attempted to carry out its mandate to promote regional economic
cooperation and integration in a number of different ways. During
the 1970s, the Bank actively promoted multicountry projects and
projects providing goods and services for the regional market.
However, most of the projects suffered from management, design,
and cost problems; inadequate marketing; lack of technical expertise; and underfunding. During the 1980s, the Bank's strategy
shifted from financing projects to the provision of technical assistance grants to carry out regional studies and training programs.

Despite the lack of success of regional projects, the CDB has
helped regional integration by giving priority to the promotion of
economic growth in the smaller countries. In 1970, the low level of
development in the LDCs was seen as an obstacle to regional integration due to the perceived uneven distribution of the gains from
liberalizing regional trade. The CDB was seen as an institution that
could provide benefits to the LDCs at low or no cost to the MDCs
and thereby foster more meaningful cooperation. Today the
process of integration has developed further among the LDCs than
among the MDCs, and income disparities between the two groups
of countries are much reduced. In fact the situation is somewhat
reversed, and living standards are now higher in some of the LDCs
than in the MDCs.

The CDB is recognized under the treaty establishing CARI-
COM as an associate institution, and it works closely with the
CARICOM and OECS secretariats in promoting regional issues.
The Bank supported the work of the West Indian Commission,
chaired by Sir Shridath Ramphal, which made a number of recommendations for furthering integration.[1] The commission consulted
widely, and its report, *Time for Action*, provides comprehensive
documentation and analysis of a wide range of subjects. The main
thrust of the economic proposals is that the region must remain
export-oriented, adopt policies necessary to become competitive,
and move towards the establishment of a common currency and a

single market economy. The commission tackled head-on a well-known weakness in CARICOM—its inability to implement decisions—and recommended the creation of institutions with political responsibility for CARICOM affairs. Specifically, the commission proposed the appointment of a council of ministers to guide and direct a CARICOM commission that would be the implementing agency for the community. The secretariat would continue in its present capacity to undertake research and analysis, and the secretary-general would be a member of the commission.

In October 1992, the governments of the region made a number of decisions supporting the move towards a single market economy. The Common External Tariff and improved rules of origin were approved, and, as a step towards the creation of a regional capital market, arrangements were made for cross-listing and cross-trading on the stock exchanges of Barbados, Jamaica, and Trinidad and Tobago. However, the heads of government did not agree to establish new institutions. The work of the commission showed that there is widespread support for closer cooperation, and, while the machinery for implementation remains weak, the process appears irreversible.

Note

1. Other supporters were the governments of the Netherlands, United Kingdom, Norway, CIDA, UNDP, the Swedish International Development Agency (SIDA), and the Commonwealth Fund for Technical Cooperation.

8

RELATIONS WITH
THE OTHER MDBS

In addition to carrying out the obligations of its Charter, the CDB
has another important function; to collaborate with the World
Bank and the IDB to promote the development of the region. To
date, World Bank and IDB lending to the Caribbean has only
involved the CDB to a limited extent, but this relationship is
changing. The CDB is expected to play a larger role in the development assistance strategy for the region in the future.

IBRD/IDA Role in the Region

Between 1980 and 1990, the World Bank group made loans
amounting to $685 million, including $53.2 million in IDA credits
to the Commonwealth Caribbean region. This amounted to about
$70 million per annum, compared with $40 million per annum by
the CDB. Most of the loans went to the MDCs; resources were
transferred to the OECS countries through the CDB until 1982
when the World Bank began to lend directly to some of these countries as well. During the 1970s, the World Bank financed projects in
the agricultural, transport, power, and education sectors, but since
1980, the lending has been primarily to support structural adjustment. The emphasis on policy reforms is likely to continue, but the
volume of future lending in the region will be constrained by IBRD
and IDA graduation policies and the high cost of operations.

The administrative costs of the World Bank's lending to the
Caribbean are relatively high due to the large number of countries,
their size, the smallness of projects, and the extensive economic
work required of the World Bank in its role as chair of the aid

group in support of policy-based lending. Over the past four years, more than forty economic reports were prepared for twelve countries in the Caribbean at a total cost of $8.6 million, or $2.15 million per annum—one-quarter of the CDB's administrative budget. It is also costly for the World Bank to keep a large staff assigned to the Caribbean region, given the low volume of lending compared to other regions.

Between 1970 and 1990, the World Bank group made five loans to the CDB totalling $96.6 million. There were two loans in the mid-1970s totalling $51 million, and two small IDA credits during the 1980s of $13.6 million. The fifth loan in 1990 was for $32 million ($20 million IBRD and $12 million IDA) at the standard terms: seventeen years maturity with five years' grace at the IBRD variable interest rate, and 40 years maturity with ten years' grace for the IDA credit. (See Table 8.1.)

Table 8.1   World Bank/IDA/EEC Lending to the CDB (in millions of dollars)

	IBRD	IDA	Third Window	EEC
1976	17.0	—	3.0	—
1978	23.0	7.0	—	1.0
1983	—	6.8	—	—
1987	—	6.8	—	—
1990	20.0	12.0	—	—

Source: World Bank.

The CDB on-lends the funds to finance projects in IBRD/IDA-eligible countries at interest rates reflecting its own costs. This rate is currently 7.5 percent plus 1 percent front-end fee, and the maturities are determined on project grounds. IDA funds are blended with IBRD funds for loans to eligible OECS countries, while Guyana receives only IDA resources. Borrowing countries may relend IDA credits at commercial rates, and the benefits of the concessionary funds accrue to the government. The foreign exchange risk is carried by governments and borrowers. The World Bank's evaluation of four fully disbursed loans showed mixed but mostly good results.

In approving the 1990 loan, the World Bank cited the CDB's strong capital structure and financial position and the fact that its sector policy and lending strategy papers were similar to those of the World Bank for the region. The CDB's project appraisal procedures and supervision were considered good, but it was felt that greater attention should be given to the institutional and environmental aspects, and projects needed to be better linked to sector policies. The appraisal report also noted that Caribbean governments, particularly those in the OECS, considered the CDB their own development agency familiar with local conditions; they wanted the CDB to play a larger role in their development, but in order to do this "the CDB would have to be able to offer competitive services and terms of financing, and develop the necessary staff experience." Another conclusion of the report was that the CDB "performs an important advisory role but has not assumed a central role in macro-policy advice, aid coordination, or regional cooperation."

The World Bank's fifth loan to the CDB in 1990 marked a departure from the previous lender/creditor relationship and envisaged a more collaborative association. For mutual advantage, the relationship was broadened to include collaboration in undertaking country economic evaluations, aid coordination, investment, adjustment-lending, and technical assistance. The new relationship is set out in a *Memorandum of Understanding* (World Bank, 1990) that states that "the CDB will complement and eventually supplant some current Bank roles in the region in areas where the CDB has a comparative advantage over the Bank. This will enable the Bank over a three to five year period to redirect its manpower resources for policy advice, support of policy reforms and other developmental work including those areas of project lending where it has the comparative advantage."

The memorandum envisages that in the future, the CDB will do adjustment lending in association with the World Bank and will do all the investment lending in the U.K.–dependent territories and the OECS. The World Bank will lend directly to the OECS only if the CDB has no processing capacity and the countries want IBRD funds. Within this framework, the CDB will continue to prepare the economic reports of the U.K.-dependent territories and the PSIPs for the OECS and Belize, while the World Bank will focus on the larger countries.

The staff of the World Bank believe that both institutions would improve the efficiency of their operations if the CDB took over some of the functions of the World Bank, particularly in the OECS countries, because this would enable the World Bank to allocate its resources to more cost-effective activities. Lending through the CDB will enable IBRD/IDA to support small projects that would otherwise be too costly to administer. As the memorandum states, "Because of its lower costs per operation, the CDB can make a larger number of loans in the region; IBRD, due to limitations of staff, would have to limit itself to fewer loans and credits in the same period. By channelling its resources through the CDB, the [World] Bank can have a broader sector/country coverage than it could making direct loans. The [World] Bank would help to strengthen the CDB both financially and institutionally to progressively take over some [World] Bank functions in the region."

The relationship between the World Bank and the CDB has been good, but it could be strengthened in several areas. The two institutions do not always agree, but they have high regard for the professionalism and integrity of the other's staff. For example, the World Bank has argued that the CDB's design of feeder roads is too expensive because it includes provision for road paving unlike feeder roads in Paraguay and Africa. The CDB has countered that the examples cited in Paraguay and Africa are not applicable to the topography of the Caribbean and that the more expensive designs are needed to protect roads and embankments from being washed away by heavy rainfall. This dispute will only be settled after project completion reports (PCRs) indicate the condition of the roads after five years. This project was to be financed with World Bank funds; to avoid delays in the processing of projects, the CDB plans to submit projects to the Board of Directors for approval with alternative sources of financing.

The CDB can become a greater channel of World Bank funds to the region, but there are a number of policies, including the cost of funds and disbursement practices, that must be reviewed. The World Bank lends to the CDB at the retail rate, and the CDB has to charge a markup. Most borrowers find that the CDB's lending rate is too high, and they prefer to look for other sources of funds. The CDB is also constrained by the World Bank's disbursement procedures. The World Bank disburses expensive hard currencies, and borrowers have to repay in the currency disbursed or the U.S. dollar, whichever the World Bank requests. This method of passing on the foreign exchange risk always assures the World Bank a profit, and borrowers have complained that this practice is unduly burdensome. The example was cited of a country that borrowed $3 million, had repaid $2 million, and still owed $2 million due to the currencies used by the World Bank. The CDB staff also find that World Bank procedures for approval are cumbersome and lengthy. Other obstacles are the World Bank's views on graduation, which would prevent BMCs from using IDA funds and even IBRD funds, and the failure of the World Bank to revise its policy that prevents the CDB from attending the Bank/IMF annual meeting.[1]

The OECS countries are not eligible for IDA credits, but they are not yet creditworthy for IBRD loans; during the transition period, most of them are receiving a 50/50 blend of IBRD/IDA funds through the CDB. Of the MDCs, the Bahamas and Barbados have graduated, Guyana can qualify for IDA funds only, and further lending to Jamaica is limited by the high level of its multilateral debt. Trinidad and Tobago is currently the largest borrower. A reduced role for the World Bank in the Caribbean makes sense from the point of view of reducing the World Bank's operating costs, but the World Bank's withdrawal also creates a number of problems. Net transfers to the region are negative, and there is no alternative official or commercial lender. Despite relatively high levels of income, the region's economies are characterized by their weak economic structures, large pockets of poverty, and the need for high levels of capital inflows. The CDB does not have the resources to replace the World Bank and can only partially fill this gap.

Relations with the IDB

The IDB is currently the largest lender to the Caribbean region (about $200 million per annum), and most of its loans go to the five countries that are IDB members: Bahamas, Barbados, Guyana, Jamaica, and Trinidad and Tobago. Six independent countries among the LDCs are eligible for membership: Antigua and Barbuda, Dominica, Grenada, St. Kitts-Nevis, St. Lucia, and St. Vincent and the Grenadines, but they have not joined. In 1974 an amendment to IDB's charter was approved that allowed the bank to "finance the development of any of the members of the CDB by providing loans and technical assistance to that institution," but IDB has made very little use of the CDB to channel resources to the OECS countries.

The IDB has had only two operations with the CDB. The first loan was made in 1978 for $12 million, and a second loan of $20 million was made in 1985. Both loans had maturities of twenty-five years, concessionary interest rates, and were on-lent by the CDB to the LDCs. IDB has also provided technical assistance grants through the CDB to regional institutions such as the CARICOM secretariat, Caribbean Tourist Organization (CTO), and the Caribbean Association of Industry and Commerce. The CDB receives a 1 percent fee for the technical grants that it administers and adds a spread on IDB lines of credit that it on-lends. Recently, the IDB has relaxed the conditionality on its lines of credit. The supervision of subprojects no longer has to be carried out by IDB staff. The audits done by the CDB's auditors are acceptable to IDB.

There is a 1978 Memorandum of Understanding between the IDB and the CDB, and both institutions try to define their roles in the region by following mutual programming strategies and identifying special areas of interest. Every year, the IDB and the CDB have coordinated meetings at the managerial, operational, and programming levels. The CDB does not finance projects over a certain size, and the IDB has a strong interest in financing projects in the social sectors. Overall, the IDB's relationship with the CDB has been limited and somewhat at arm's length, but this is beginning to change. The IDB staff feel that the relationship between the two agencies has matured, and the CDB is no longer considered just a financial intermediary but a valuable partner pursuing the same broad goals as the IDB in the region.

In 1992, the IDB prepared a regional strategy paper for the Caribbean that recognized that such a strategy could only be implemented through the CDB because several members of CARICOM were not members of the IDB. Alternatively, the OECS countries will be forced to consider membership in the IDB in order to gain access to its resources, but this would not be cost-effective for the IDB or the OECS countries. However, a number of operational and technical problems need to be addressed before the CDB could become the channel for increased IDB lending to the region.

The IDB's concessional resources are available only to category D countries. Guyana is the only one such among the CDB's borrowers, and this restricts the volume of concessional resources that the IDB could make available to the CDB and the OECS countries. The IDB has also established an Intermediate Financial Facility (IFF) to subsidize interest (by 5 percent per annum) to all category C countries; it will increase the level of financing to 70 percent of project costs for category C countries and 80 percent for category D countries. The CDB's current lending rate of 7.5 percent per annum limits its ability to cofinance projects with the IDB from its ordinary capital resources. In 1992, the IDB made a loan of $56 million to UWI that was guaranteed by the governments of Jamaica, Trinidad and Tobago, and Barbados and cofinanced by the CDB. The IDB financed 70 percent of the project costs. UWI met the other 30 percent by borrowing $9 million from the CDB. The IDB loan utilized the IFF and carried an interest rate of only 3 percent. The CDB loan utilized special fund resources.

A major issue for the World Bank, the IDB, and other lenders is how to sustain a net flow of resources to the region during a prolonged period of adjustment. All the MDCs are carrying out World Bank/IMF–sponsored structural adjustment programs and are struggling with very difficult socioeconomic problems. The LDCs are highly vulnerable to the fluctuations in world demand and prices and to natural disasters. Greater attention also needs to be given to promoting a regional development strategy to respond to changes taking place in global trading arrangements. Both the World Bank and the IDB have indicated a willingness to collaborate more closely with the CDB, but they need to make the institutional strengthening of the CDB an important component of their regional development strategy.

The procedures for collaboration must be standardized to ensure that the CDB does not operate three different sets of reporting requirements, disbursements, and lending policies relating to its own loans and the on-lending of World Bank and IDB loans. Careful attention must also be given to the speed with which responsibility is handed over to the CDB for economic work and new areas of lending, because these new activities will raise the Bank's operating costs and stretch its tight staff resources.

Finally, the financial relationship between the agencies must be restructured so that the World Bank and the IDB lend to the CDB at a rate lower than the current lending rate to their borrowers; the loans must not count against the callable capital of the CDB because they are already guaranteed by the shareholders of the larger MDBs and would otherwise restrict the CDB's ability to borrow on its own account.

Note

1. In 1980 a decision was made banning the Palestine Liberation Organization from attending the World Bank/IMF annual meeting. All other agencies with observer status were banned as well. Since that time CDB senior staff could only attend the annual meeting by arranging to join one of the member country delegations. In 1993 the CDB followed suit by not inviting the World Bank to its annual meeting.

9

LOOMING DEVELOPMENT CHALLENGES FOR THE BANK

The CDB has been successful both as a financial and a development institution. The Bank began operations in 1970 with an authorized capital of $50 million and a paid-in share of $25 million. In 1991, its financial resources amounted to almost $1 billion, and it had an accumulated net income of $70 million. During the 1980s, the Bank experienced a large buildup of arrears, but these were mainly on loans to Guyana. In 1990, the CDB worked closely with the World Bank, the IMF, and several bilateral donors on an Economic Recovery Program for Guyana that resulted in the clearance of these arrears.

In 1990, the Board of Governors approved a general capital increase of $200 million; and in 1991 negotiations were completed on the replenishment of the SDF at $124 million for 1992–1995. In 1992, the CDB received a triple-A rating from Moody's Investors Service and made its first borrowing of $30 million in the U.S. private placement market. These events signalled recognition by the international financial community of the CDB's stable record of prudent financial policies and sound management. The CDB's financial ratios compare favorably with those of the other MDBs, and the prospects for its continued viability are good.

The CDB enjoys the confidence and strong backing of its members. They have supported all the requests for general capital increases since 1970, and their capital subscriptions have always been made on time. Some members have even paid-in their subscriptions in advance. The current level of paid-in capital is 22.1 percent, which is much higher than for other MDBs.

As a development institution, the CDB has had a positive impact on economic development in the Caribbean region through the provision of loans, technical assistance grants, and policy advice. Regional members have also benefited from their share of procurement contracts, which was as much as 72 percent in 1990. The CDB has further helped to promote increased economic cooperation within the region and between Latin America and the Caribbean. Colombia, Venezuela, and Mexico have provided financial resources through the CDB for regional development.

The CDB is important to the region due to the continuity of its staff, who are from the region, know the senior government officials well, and can influence decisionmakers. The senior staff have been with the CDB for ten to twenty years, whereas World Bank staff change frequently. (Over the past decade and a half, there has been a procession of five vice-presidents, five directors, and four division chiefs in charge of Latin America and the Caribbean in the World Bank.) The staff of the CDB have built up special skills in dealing with the range of economic, engineering, financial, and institutional problems affecting projects in the region; they participate in economic policy discussions, and, due to their proximity and knowledge, they are able to operate in a manner better adapted to the political and economic conditions in member countries.

The CDB has played a modest but important role in the mobilization of resources for investment. Overall, the Bank has financed only 6 percent of the public sector investments in the region, but in the OECS countries, its share of the financing has been as high as 40 percent. The CDB did not have the financial resources to provide balance-of-payments assistance to cushion the fall in imports or to make social sector loans to alleviate poverty; nor did it have the staff resources for policy-based lending. It focused instead on small project loans to build the regions' infrastructure and to strengthen the development finance companies that were the principal source of funds to the small-scale private sector.

The sectoral distribution of its loans reflects the investment priorities of the region. Infrastructure development accounted for 40 percent of loan approvals. The projects to build feeder roads; extend and rehabilitate main roads, ports, and airports; increase the supply of power; and improve the availability of clean water and sewerage facilities have been successful. "It is in infrastructure where the CDB has made its mark and enhanced the absorptive capacity and productive capabilities of its members."[1] The overall performance of the CDB's project portfolio has been strong, with more than half of the projects under supervision experiencing moderate or no problems. In addition to project funding, the CDB has been very successful in strengthening the operational and financial management of the public utilities in the power, ports, and water sectors, especially in the LDCs. Through its technical assistance programs, the Bank has also made a major contribution to building institutions and to increasing the supply of skilled personnel able to identify and prepare investment projects.

The CDB has had an important qualitative impact on economic policies beyond the resources it has made available. It has helped to strengthen fiscal discipline and to raise the quality of public administration in several borrowing countries. In the early 1970s, the LDCs were in receipt of budgetary support from the United Kingdom. When this support was withdrawn, these countries experienced severe fiscal difficulties. Today most of these countries are registering budgetary surpluses. In summarizing the role the CDB has played, Sir Neville Nichols recalled the comment of Sir Arthur Lewis that "whoever can teach financial discipline to the OECS states will deserve a prize."[2]

The CDB is an efficient and well-managed institution. There has been a steady decrease in the staff since 1980, the cost of preparing projects has fallen, and the administrative budget has shown little or no increase in real terms over the past five years. As a result, the CDB has developed into a strong project-lending institution whose professional staff is highly regarded and whose project processing is faster and less costly than that of the IDB and the World Bank.

The Bank has carried out its mandate to give priority to the LDCs, which received 55 percent of its total lending and 90 percent of its technical assistance grants. The high rates of economic growth of the LDCs over the past decade have contributed to the strength of its project portfolio. Until recently, the Bank has had a much smaller role in the MDCs. Jamaica is the largest borrower of ordinary capital resources, and it has been able to obtain concessional funds for project implementation and for hurricane rehabilitation. During the 1980s, Barbados and Trinidad and Tobago had little need of the CDB's resources, and lending to Guyana was precluded due to its arrears.

Country studies and project evaluation reports indicate that the CDB has been a key partner in the economic development of Belize and the OECS countries (especially Dominica, St. Kitts-Nevis, St. Lucia, and St. Vincent and the Grenadines) by providing significant funding for the infrastructure and the productive sectors as well as technical assistance and consultancy services in financial management and public sector investment. The CDB has also provided significant benefits to Jamaica and Barbados.

Overview of Strategy to Year 2000

After the compliments, it must be added that the CDB cannot rest on its accomplishments. It must continually adapt and innovate in order to be an active participant and leader in the region's development and to become more efficient in its lending operations. It must develop new approaches to appraisal and supervision of projects in order to reduce costs, as well as to develop new forms of financing and new sectors of support. Staff must be recruited and trained for these shifts. In order to plan its future lending strategy, the CDB carried out a management and productivity study in 1990 to identify areas where efficiency, effectiveness, and productivity could be improved; it also hosted a symposium entitled "The CDB to the Year 2000."

These activities were inputs into the directional plan/strategy for the year 2000, which stated that during the 1990s, the CDB proposes to exploit more fully, in support of its borrowers, its strength in project financing; its advantage in local knowledge; its good relations with IFIs, donor, and regional governments; and its ability to mobilize resources. The plan had the following goals:

a. to strengthen the economic work and intensify the policy dialogue with borrowers and donors;
b. to mobilize additional resources to expand the lending program at 5 percent per annum in real terms;
c. to increase lending for human resource development, environmental protection, and public health;
d. to provide assistance for capital market development and institution building;
e. to support policy reform through increased sector lending; and
f. to increase the supervision of problem projects and institutions.

The plan also reaffirmed the CDB's commitment to maintain prudent financial management. The stated financial goals in the directional plan included earning a net income of 7 percent of usable equity; maintaining liquidity sufficient to cover 40 percent of undisbursed loan commitments; keeping administrative expenses to 1.6 percent of loans outstanding; and increasing the ratio of disbursed to undisbursed loans.

In sum, no major shifts in lending strategies are envisaged over the medium term, but greater attention will be given to private sector development and assessing the environmental impact of projects. However, as indicated in the recent loans to the petroleum sector in Trinidad, for sugar rehabilitation in Barbados, and the joint IDB loan to the University of the West Indies, both the country and sectoral composition of the lending program are likely to change in response to shifts in the types of resources available to the CDB and the special needs of the borrowers.

For purposes of determining eligibility for the CDB's concessional resources, most of which goes to Group 3 countries, the CDB has adopted a country classification scheme other than simply the MDC/LDC one, as follows:

- Group 1: Bahamas, Barbados, Cayman Islands, and Trinidad and Tobago
- Group 2: Anguilla, Antigua and Barbuda, British Virgin Islands
- Group 3: Other OECS and Jamaica
- Group 4: Guyana

Issues to Address

The region faces a number of formidable challenges arising out of the sluggish growth in the industrial countries, the potential loss of preferential export markets, and declining capital inflows. On the domestic front, borrowing countries must restore the competitiveness of their exports and tackle the problems of growing poverty, unemployment, and environmental damage. The countries of the region have always shown great resilience in adjusting to rapid changes in the global economy. Sustained growth will require not only the formulation of development strategies that take these changes into account but much higher levels of investment to finance the needed changes in the structure of output.

Low Investment

The working-age population is expected to expand faster than the number of new jobs due to the youthful age-structure of the population. The region needs high rates of GDP growth to keep unemployment from rising. Many countries are implementing stabilization and adjustment programs that involve a larger role for the private sector and a more supportive role for the public sector, but these programs will not be sufficient to stimulate growth without a steady increase in net capital flows to finance higher levels of investment.

Current levels of investment are constrained because aid flows to the region have been declining. Many highly indebted borrowers (Jamaica, Guyana, Trinidad and Tobago, Barbados, and Grenada) are unable to increase their net borrowing from the IFIs and commercial banks. At the same time, budget stringency limits the ability of governments to finance needed improvements in the social and economic infrastructure and to cushion the adverse impact of adjustment policies on the poor. Declining capital flows to the region will increase the importance of the CDB as a new source of long-term capital mobilization.

Poverty and Unemployment

Poverty in the region increased during the 1980s, particularly in Guyana and Trinidad, where malnutrition was the leading cause of death among infants, and in Jamaica where 43 percent of the population had incomes below the poverty line, according to a Survey of Living Conditions carried out in 1988. The increase in poverty is related to the high rates of unemployment among prime-age workers. Official statistics indicate that the average unemployment rate in the region is 20 percent, and for some of the smaller countries, it is 30 percent or higher. The unemployment rate among women is often double the rate for men and is also very high among young people. Growing levels of unemployment and poverty are socially destabilizing.

Education

The alleviation of poverty and unemployment will require increased spending on education. Most governments spend 26–30 percent of government revenue on the provision of education, but, during the 1980s, a number of countries experienced a marked deterioration in educational standards due to budget cuts and the shortage of qualified teachers. Tests in Jamaica indicate that 30 percent of the primary school-leavers are functionally illiterate. A very small percentage of the region's school-leavers get a postsecondary education. Greater attention needs to be given to the appropriateness of the curricula, teacher training and quality, cost recovery, and the involvement of the private sector.

Increased spending on education must take into account the high rates of emigration of the most educated and highly trained workers. The loss of skilled workers in Jamaica during 1980–1986 was equal to 50 percent of the graduates produced, and a recent survey in Trinidad indicated that 75 percent of the nurses planned to emigrate. The migration of professionals places a heavy burden on the budget and reduces the skill-mix of the remaining work-force. Efforts must be made to encourage host countries, institutions, and migrants to contribute to the costs of improved quality of, and access to, education. Hospitals in North America, for example, could be asked to share the costs of training health care professionals in the Caribbean.

Environmental Degradation

There is increasing awareness in the region of the severity of the damage being done to the environment, and most of the problems can be traced to economic causes. The use of fertilizers and pesticides contributes to the pollution of rivers and streams, and the expansion of the acreage under cultivation and the growth of squatter settlements are leading to deforestation. The average marine catch declined sharply in the OECS countries during the 1980s due to overfishing, and coastal zone degradation is a problem in Antigua, Dominica, Grenada, St. Kitts, St. Lucia, and St. Vincent. The beaches are threatened by disposal of sewage and other wastes into the ocean, by sand mining for construction, and by the destruction of coral reefs. But the most common cause of water pollution and coastal erosion is inadequate waste management. This includes inadequate sewage disposal, inadequate solid and liquid waste disposal, and the unchecked disposal of industrial and toxic waste in local waters.

The governments of the region and the CDB do not have the resources to address these environmental problems. They must coordinate their efforts with those of the multilateral and bilateral agencies that are making environmental assessments and financing projects. However, the CDB has to do more to disseminate information on the magnitude of the problem, to establish regional environmental policies and a strong regulatory framework, and to take the environmental aspects into account in its project lending.

Priorities for Lending _____

In the future the CDB will stick to its main area of strength, which is project lending; priority will be given to increased lending for agriculture, tourism, and human resource development. The Bank will continue to provide infrastructure support for tourism and is expected to lend more for the improvement of water and sanitation facilities and assist countries in the development of knowledge-based industries. The average size of projects is increasing. This will undoubtedly reduce operational costs, but it also means making fewer loans and lending to fewer countries each year.

The CDB will continue to assist in the development of the private sector through direct and indirect lending, and it will explore the possibilities of joint operations with the IFC. The CDB is allowed by its Charter to take equity positions and to lend to the private sector without a government guarantee, but it has long had a policy of requiring government guarantees or adequate security for its private sector loans. The current policy is to limit direct lending to the private sector to $5 million per annum (10 percent of OCR lending). Indirect lending to the private sector through the DFCs accounts for 20–25 percent of the total lending. The CDB needs to do more to attract private investment to the region and to promote the growth of regional capital markets.

In recognition of the global trend towards the formation of economic and trading blocs, the CDB has been asked by its Board of Governors to play a greater role in regional development. The Bank's efforts to support regional projects during the 1970s met with little success. The grain projects in Guyana and Belize were well designed but ran into financial and managerial difficulties. The livestock and fisheries projects were overdesigned and needed more technical and managerial skills than were available locally. The projects to improve regional transportation failed primarily due to the lack of capital. The CDB feels that the governments did not give these projects the support they needed, but, if the lack of capital and skilled labor were the major problems, this is evidence of the severity of the resource constraints and not a lack of support.

The CDB should allocate a part of its lending program to financing projects that will enhance regional production possibilities and promote intraregional trade. Economic integration is essential to the long-term growth of its borrowers, and regional projects are not in the lending programs of the other MDBs. Local manufacturers need to build a strong base in the regional market to improve their competitiveness, and the traders in the informal economy who are spearheading integration need access to credit. The CDB should focus on a particular sector or activity and finance a regional project every two years, because the ability to cooperate has its own learning curve.

Although the scope for making structural adjustment loans is limited by the lack of resources, the CDB is expected to play a larger role in macro- and sector-adjustment lending in conjunction with the World Bank and the IDB. The Bank must be selective in developing areas of expertise, and it must act as a broker to the IFIs and donor community in articulating the priorities and sensitivities of the region. In its lending and economic work, the Bank intends to help governments to reduce their direct involvement in the productive sectors and to increase spending on social and economic infrastructure. Governments will be encouraged to enhance their capacity in setting macroeconomic policy, strengthening the regulatory framework, and improving public administration and security.

The CDB has an important role to play in ensuring the effective use of resources, but it must also be better capitalized in order to expand its lending operations. The Bank's total assets amount to $257 million, which makes the CDB 100 times smaller than the IDB and 400 times smaller than the World Bank. The capital base can be expanded through an increase in membership and regular capital increases. Regional members may have difficulty in meeting the paid-in capital subscriptions needed to maintain their majority voting rights, but this is not an insurmountable problem. The paid-in portion of future capital increases could be substantially reduced from the current level of 22 percent to 10 percent, as in the World Bank and the IDB.

Institutional Changes

In order to lay the foundation for a substantial increase in lending, the CDB needs to make a few institutional changes. The present organizational structure works well, but several departments need strengthening. The Economics and Programming Department must be equipped to exercise a leadership role in the policy dialogue to help formulate the region's long-term development strategy. A programming exercise should be conducted with the World Bank and the IDB to establish a clearer division of responsibility for analytical economic work and regional institution strengthening. The department needs to draw attention to the issues affecting the region by hosting seminars and commissioning work from regional institutions. The CDB also needs to spend more resources to disseminate information on its activities, to expand its outreach, to share its experiences, and to make available its thinking on important issues affecting the region.

Consideration should be given to reducing the size of the Board of Directors, which is quite large in relation to the size and membership of the Bank (see Table 9.1).

Table 9.1   Board of Directors

MDB	Members	Directors
World Bank	151	24
IDB	44	12
ADB	47	12
AFDB	75	18
CDB	25	17

A smaller Board of nine members (five Commonwealth Caribbean, one regional non-Commonwealth and three nonregional) would be less costly and more effective. The Canadian and U.K. directors are resident in Barbados, and nonregional directors meet as a group to discuss issues before board meetings. Regional members would benefit from similar meetings and from more time to become acquainted with the issues. Consideration should also be given to encouraging more active involvement by regional directors by moving to a rotating system of resident and nonresident directors.

The CDB's staff must remain small, highly skilled, and flexible. With the present staff of 200, the Bank could easily maintain a much larger lending program, because the average size of loans is only $5 million. The CDB has been held to a tight administrative budget for several years, and this is now counterproductive. In order to reduce costs further, the CDB appears to be moving in the direction of larger sectoral and project loans and away from the more staff-intensive project loans and institution building. Further reductions in the level of staff would adversely affect the quality of Bank operations. The budget constraints should be relaxed to enable the CDB to strengthen its economic and analytical skills, recruit specialists, and permit more training and skills upgrading.

In responding to some of the problems encountered by its borrowers and to increase operational efficiency, the CDB should consider the following changes in its operational and financial policies:

a. review the procedures that may contribute to delays in disbursement;
b. ensure that the primary responsibility for supervision is carried out by the borrowing agency/country and that the CDB's role is to provide qualitative input;
c. strengthen the internal procedures for monitoring the quality of the project portfolio;
d. provide increased technical assistance to improve project implementation;
e. adopt policies to help borrowers reduce costs from fluctuations in the currencies disbursed.

Long-term Development Strategy

The CDB has matured as a financial and development institution. It now needs to rise to a higher level of lending, play a larger role in policy dialogue, exercise intellectual leadership, and deepen its involvement in the region's development. Management must resist requests to take on too many responsibilities for economic and sector work or more diversified lending operations. Instead, the CDB should carve a niche for itself in relation to the work of the larger MDBs operating in the region and emphasize its strength in certain areas of project financing and economic analysis.

The current economic policy dialogue is dominated by consideration of stabilization and adjustment programs and the role of the private sector, but these are not long-term development strategies. Similarly, the list of topics of concern to donors (environment, poverty, governance, women) do not add up to a development policy or strategy. These initiatives need to fit into a comprehensive long-term framework for the region's development, but such a framework does not currently exist. For example, emphasis is given to enhancing the role of the private sector, but regional integration and industrialization are long-term objectives that need government support for social setup costs (infrastructure, research, marketing, and so on) and a partnership between governments and the private sector. The priority being given to human resource development will require increased public spending on investments with low-cost recovery by governments whose tax base is limited. A long-term strategy must balance these competing objectives, establish priorities, and mobilize the resources for implementation.

The CDB's most encouraging strategic new commitment is to the intensification of its "policy dialogue with borrowing member countries, other international financial institutions, donors and development institutions active in the region."[3] Relations with the other MDBs have helped the CDB to grow as a development and a financial institution, to coordinate development policy in the region, and to gain access to concessional resources from the IFIs. Sensibly, the CDB's members want the Bank to participate more actively in the policy discussions with the larger MDBs in the design of appropriate macro- and sector-adjustment policies and to coordinate its lending program with the MDBs.

Notes

1. Dwight Venner, governor of the ECCB.
2. From a speech by Sir Neville Nichols at the CDB annual meeting, Bridgetown, Barbados, May 1993.
3. Caribbean Development Bank, "Directional Plan/Strategy."

APPENDIX

Table A1 Principal Loan Terms and Conditions (as of July 1, 1993)

	Ordinary Resources	Special Resources
Interest rate	Variable interest rate reviewed annually (current 7.5%)	—
Group 1 countries	—	5%
Group 2 countries	—	4%
Group 3 countries	—	2%
Group 4 countries	—	2%
Upper loan limits		
LDC governments and Guyana	80% of project costs	90% of project cost
MDC governments	70% of project cost	80% of project cost
Private sector	40% of project cost subject to an acceptable debt/equity ratio	
Lower loan limits	U.S. $750,000	U.S. $750,000
Commitment fee	1% p.a. on undisbursed balance 60 days after loan agreement signed	—
Front-end fee	0% on public sector loans	
	1% on private sector loans	
Term and grace period		
Grace period	Up to 5 years	—
Term after grace period (industry and tourism projects)	10–15 years (15–18 years)	—
Group 1 countries	—	20 years including 5 years' grace
Group 2 countries	—	30 years including 7 years' grace
Group 3 countries	—	40 years including 10 years' grace
Group 4 countries	—	40 years including 10 years' grace
Exchange risk	Borne by borrower or guarantor	Borne by borrower or guarantor

Source: CDB documents.
Notes: Group 1: Bahamas, Barbados, Cayman Islands, Trinidad and Tobago
Group 2: Anguilla, Antigua and Barbuda, and British Virgin Islands
Group 3: OECS, Belize, Jamaica, Turks and Caicos Islands
Group 4: Guyana

Table A2   Selected Socioeconomic Indicators of the CDB's Borrowing Member Countries

Country	Area (sq. km)	Midyear Population 1990 (in hundreds)	GDP at Current Market Prices 1990 ($m)	GDP per Capita at Current Prices 1990 ($)	Central Government Current Revenue as % GDP	Central Government Current Expenditure as % GDP	Central Government Current Surplus as % GDP
MDCs (weighted average)	245,892	4,896.0	13,742.0	2,807	26.4	25.2	1.2
Bahamas	13,939	253.3	2,810.8	1,096	18.3	17.7	0.6
Barbados	431	257.4	1,710.5	6,645	27.6	27.8	(0.2)
Guyana	214,970	754.4	256.3	340	52.9	75.2	(22.4)
Jamaica	11,424	2,403.5	3,993.8	1,662	30.0	26.0	4.0
Trinidad and Tobago	5,128	1,227.4	4,970.6	4,050	26.1	25.1	1.0
LDCs (weighted average)	26,795	841.6	2,942.0	3,496	24.0	21.7	2.4
Belize	22,960	184.9	364.7	1,973	28.1	21.4	6.7
OECS (weighted average)	2,913	591.9	1,573.1	2,658	25.1	23.5	1.6
Antigua and Barbuda	442	84.0	418.7	4,985	19.8	20.2	(0.4)
Dominica	750	83.5	171.2	2,050	30.2	28.2	2.1
Grenada	345	100.2	200.4	2,000	29.3	30.6	(1.3)
Montserrat	103	12.0	73.6	6,133	19.7	19.2	0.5
St. Kitts-Nevis	269	42.9	152.7	3,560	20.7	19.9	0.8
St. Lucia	616	151.3	365.3	2,415	27.2	20.9	6.3
St. Vincent and the Grenadines	388	118.0	191.2	1,620	29.5	29.1	0.4
Other LDCs (weighted average)	922	64.8	1,004.2	15,497	20.9	18.8	2.1
Anguilla	91	8.5	50.2	5,906	25.6	23.7	1.9
British Virgin Islands	150	16.6	165.1	9,946	28.6	22.7	5.9
Cayman Islands	264	27.3	718.6	26,320	17.2	15.8	1.4
Turks and Caicos Islands	417	12.4	70.3	5,669	37.1	37.0	0.1
All countries (weighted average)	272,687	5,737.6	16,684.0	2,908	26.0	24.6	1.4

Sources: Reports of Statistical Offices, Central Banks, and the CDB.

Table A3   The CDB: Five Years at a Glance (dollar amounts in millions)

	1988	1989	1990	1991	1992	1993
Supervision						
Direct projects under supervision	255	261	265	273	299	302
Projects under implementation	69	77	87	95	118	105
Projects operational	186	184	178	178	181	197
Financial intermediaries	23	23	26	27	19	20
Administration						
Total staff in place at December 31	200	202	188	186	189	187
Total administrative expenses	6.5	6.7	7.4	8.5	9.0	9.6
Administrative expenses to total average loans outstanding (%)	1.7	1.6	1.6	1.7	1.7	1.8
Approvals						
Capital projects (new)						
Approved for loan financing	17	16	17	18	12	15
In which OCR involved	7	11	16	14	11	12
Loans approved for capital						
Projects (new and additional)	65.9	76.0	115.4	108.9	79.5	91.5
Of which OCR accounted for	12.9	43.5	51.0	72.3	52.6	45.8
Loans (net) approved for capital						
Projects (new, additional, and contingent)	65.9	73.6	101.2	108.7	70.7	70.2
Amount approved for technical assistance and grants	8.1	1.0	8.2	2.8	20.0	1.1
Disbursements						
Amount disbursed in OCR and Venezuelan Trust Fund (VTF)	24.6	20.2	21.2	20.7	27.9	22.5
Amount disbursed in SFR	33.6	38.7	66.7	33.1	33.0	25.8
Total disbursed	58.2	58.9	87.9	53.8	60.9	48.3
Net transfers	23.6	18.7	5.9	(2.1)	(1.3)	(11.1)
Portfolio						
OCR loans outstanding	132.8	143.1	155.6	165.5	177.4	188.0
VTF loans outstanding	7.2	6.5	5.6	4.8	4.1	3.4
SFR loans outstanding	263.9	288.9	343.1	349.5	348.3	346.4
Total loans outstanding	403.9	438.5	504.3	519.8	529.8	537.8
Financial performance						
Net income on OCR	6.5	6.9	25.9	12.4	13.6	12.8
Net income on SFR	4.7	8.3	16.7	7.6	6.6	4.1
Total net income	11.2	15.2	42.6	20.0	20.2	16.9

Source: CDB.

BIBLIOGRAPHY

Where a title is given in italics, it is a published document. Those in quotation marks are internal.

Blackman, Courtney N. *The Barbados-CDB Connection*, background paper, November 1992.

Caribbean Development Bank. *CDB Annual Report*, 1970 to 1993.

———. *CDB News*, 1991 to date.

———. "CDB to the Year 2000: Proceedings of the Twentieth Anniversary Symposium," May 1990.

———. "Directional Plan/Strategy: CDB to the Year 2000," December 1991.

———. *The First Ten Years, 1970–1980.*

———. *The First Twenty Years, 1970–1990.*

———. *Likely Global Trends, Possible Implications and Suggested Strategies for the Caribbean*, October 1992.

———. "Sector Policy Paper: Environment," October 1993.

———. "Sector Policy Paper: Human Resource Development," November 1993.

———. "Speeches by the President," June 1992–March 1993.

———. "Statements by the Presidents," 1971–1980.

———. "Statements by the Presidents," 1980–1989.

———. "Work Programme and Administrative Budget," 1992.

CARICOM Secretariat. "International Conference on Financing Caribbean Agricultural Development," 1991.

Chaney, Elsa. *Scenarios of Hunger in the Caribbean*, Michigan State University, 1983.

Cleveland, Alfred S., and Athans, Paul. *Survey Report of the Feasibility of Establishing a Caribbean Regional Development Bank to USAID*, California: Stanford Research Institute, 1963.

Commonwealth Secretariat. *Caribbean Development to the Year 2000*, London 1988.

———. *Guyana: The Economic Recovery Programme and Beyond, Report of the Commonwealth Advisory Group*, London, August 1989.

Demas, William G. *Towards West Indian Survival*, West Indian Commission Secretariat, Barbados 1992.

Economist Intelligence Unit. *Country Profile, Guyana, Barbados, Windward and Leeward Islands*, 1992–1993.

Ferguson, James. *Far from Paradise*, London: Latin American Bureau, 1990.

119

Girvan, Norman. *Caribbean Integration: Rhetoric or Reality?* Sixth ILO Conference, Mona, Jamaica, March 1991.

Harrison, Graham. *Towards a Better Understanding of Trade Liberalization as It Relates to the Commonwealth Caribbean,* Caribbean Development Bank, October 1992.

Humes, Dorla. *The Caribbean Economy: Problems and Prospects in the Age of Restructuring,* Caribbean Development Bank, May 1992.

International Monetary Fund, "Barbados—Recent Economic Developments," June 1992.

————. "Guyana, Staff Report," October 1991, February 1994.

————. "Jamaica, Staff Report," March 1992, September 1993.

Lewis, W. Arthur, "The Slowing Down of the Engine of Growth," *American Economic Review* 70, no. 4, September 1980.

Marshall, Ione. *Barbados and the CDB,* background paper, August 1992.

Moore, Fauzya. *CARICOM: The Road Between,* North-South Institute, Ottawa, April 1992.

Muir, Rudolph. *Structural Adjustment in the Nineties,* Caribbean Development Bank, June 1992.

Pastor, Robert. *Migration and Development in the Caribbean,* Boulder, Colorado: Westview Press, 1985.

Reid, George. *Jamaica's Relations with the CDB 1970–1992,* North-South Institute, 1995.

St. Rose, Marius. *The CDB as an Instrument for Promoting Economic Cooperation and Development,* Caribbean Development Bank, July 1990.

Singh, Sharon A. *Report of a Mission to St. Kitts-Nevis, St. Lucia, St. Vincent and Grenada,* April 1992.

The West Indian Commission Secretariat. *Statistical Profile of the Caribbean Community,* compiled by Ione Marshall, 1992.

————. *Time for Action,* Barbados, 1992.

Williams, Eric. "Debt, Adjustment and Development: Looking to the Nineties," Memorial Lecture, Central Bank, Trinidad and Tobago, May 1990.

World Bank. *The Caribbean Common Market: Trade Policies and Regional Integration in the 1990s,* December 1990.

————. *Caribbean Countries: Policies for Private Sector Development,* March 1994.

————. *Caribbean Region: Coping with Changes in the External Environment,* April 1994.

————. *Caribbean Region, Current Economic Situation, Regional Issues and Capital Flows,* April 1992.

————. *Economic Policies for Transition in the OECS,* February 1994.

————. *Economic Reports: St. Vincent and the Grenadines, Grenada, St. Lucia, St. Kitts-Nevis,* February 1990.

————. *Long-Term Economic Prospects of the OECS Countries,* February 1990.

————. "Staff Appraisal Report," Fifth CDB Project, March 1990.

————. "Staff Appraisal Report," Sixth CDB Project, March 1994.

Worrell, Delisle, Compton Bourne, and Dinesh Dodhia, eds. *Financing Development in the Commonwealth Caribbean,* London: Commonwealth Secretariat, 1991.

INDEX

ABOUT THE BOOK
AND AUTHOR

The multilateral banks are powerful forces in the international community, providing loans of more than $250 billion to developing countries over the last half-century. The best-known of these, the World Bank, has been studied extensively, but the "regional development banks" are little understood, even within their own geographic regions.

This book looks specifically at the policies and projects of the Caribbean Development Bank, which, like the other multilateral banks, is being scrutinized increasingly by grassroots organizations, environmental groups, and others.

Drawing on case studies, Hardy responds to some basic questions: Has the Caribbean Development Bank in fact been an effective agent of development? Has it been a mere clone of the World Bank, susceptible to that agency's weaknesses, as well as its strengths? She also assesses the bank's ability to take on the emerging challenges on the development agenda, including such issues as governance and the need for gender-sensitive development strategies.

Chandra Hardy is an associate of the International Development Training Institute in Washington, D.C. She worked from 1967 to 1988 in various posts at the World Bank in Washington, D.C., most recently as senior economist in the Asian region.